As You Like It

As You Like It

As Directed by
John Hirsch
Edited by
Elliott Hayes
and
Michal Schonberg

CBC Enterprises/les Entreprises Radio-Canada

MONTRÉAL • TORONTO • NEW YORK • LONDON

Published by CBC Enterprises/les Entreprises Radio-Canada, a division of the Canadian Broadcasting Corporation, Box 500, Station A, Toronto (Ontario), Canada M5W 1E6, in association with The Stratford Shakespearean Festival Foundation of Canada, Box 520, Stratford (Ontario), Canada N5A 6V2.

Publié par CBC Enterprises/les Entreprises Radio-Canada, une division de la Société Radio-Canada, C.P. 500, Succursale «A», Toronto (Ontario), Canada M5W 1E6, en collaboration avec la Stratford Shakespearean Festival Foundation of Canada, C.P. 520, Stratford (Ontario), Canada N5A 6V2.

The CBC television production of *As You Like It* was filmed in 1983. The Producer was Sam Levene and the Director was Herb Roland.

CANADIAN CATALOGUING IN PUBLICATION DATA

Shakespeare, William, 1564-1616.
  As you like it

Stratford Festival ed.
ISBN 0-88794-118-4

I. Title.
PR2803.A1 1983   822.3'3   C83-098567-0

General Manager/Directeur général: Guy R. Mazzeo
Publisher/Éditeur: Glenn Edward Witmer
Editor/Révision: Betty Corson
Designer/Conception graphique: Leslie Smart and Associates Limited
Typesetter/Composition: CompuScreen Typesetting Limited
Printer/Impression: D. W. Friesen and Sons Limited

Printed and bound in Canada

1   2   3   4   5   /   87   86   85   84   83

Distributed to the trade by:
Macmillan of Canada (a division of Gage Publishing Limited), Toronto

Contents

The Director's Views on
As You Like It

(given to the full company at first rehearsal)

By John Hirsch

It is always an awesome time and moment when we begin a season. The material that we work on – thank God – is always marvellous. It has stood the test of time. What you do with it, bringing your own souls and your own talents and your own energies and your own intellect to it, is what will make this season different, what will make a different production of whatever play we are doing. In this case, it is *As You Like It*.

I ought to talk to you about the various elements in this play that appeal to me, elements I have loved and worked with and forever enjoy uncovering. First of all, it is a fairy tale. As you know, fairy tales are very serious things because they deal with myths. They deal with subconscious matters – deep-running, underground rivers whose rumblings are forever there in our lives but not articulated as often as they are in fairy tales. Basically, they deal with good and evil. They are a guide for children at a very early age as to how the world is and how to live and how to cope with things. And fairy tales are full of archetypal images – people who play out these eternal problems of good and evil. This play doesn't have, in my opinion, as comprehensive and unified a pattern as *The Tempest*, but it deals with many of the same elements that make all of Shakespeare's fairy tales so rich.

Now what are these elements? First, it is a romance, a comedy, which means that it starts with death and it ends with life, with regeneration: Even in the tragedies there is always that tiny glimpse of regeneration, rebirth, hope – whatever you want to call it. All the comedies, all the romances, end somehow at the height of Summer, where the bounty of God – and above all, Nature – is in front of you to give you hope, to give you an understanding, an affirmation. So this is an essential pattern for this play: To go from Winter through Spring to Summer to Harvest and the celebration of the Harvest – the celebration of unity, which takes the form of a masque. That's the culmination of the whole play.

Another important element is the archetypal pattern that occurs in all the romances: It is impossible to remain in the city, in the middle of what is called civilization, and find yourself. So you have to run away. Most rulers in Shakespeare, Samson-like, pull down the very edifice they support and which supports them, bringing this apparent disaster upon themselves so they can be exiled in order to find themselves. Prospero becomes such a lousy, rotten ruler, locking himself in his library, that there is nothing to be done with him except put him out to sea. He wants to be exiled; he wants to get away to learn about himself. In *As You Like It* Duke Senior and all of these dukes are exiled, but I bet dollars to donuts that they want to get out, except they can't say, "I'm resigning, ladies and gentlemen, so get yourselves another Duke. Good-bye." They can't say it because they're infected with the idea of power. But subconsciously they are smart enough to keep cutting away at the pillars of their own Parthenon. And then when it falls down, they can run and they can blame it on the society. The point is, however, that they always wanted to run away to find out who they are and what they are.

Another element in *As You Like It* has to do with the ongoing conflict in Western society between the man-made world and Nature: Which is better for us human beings? It's an irresolvable conflict; but, over and over again, in the history of Western civilization, romantic movements emerge, prompting people to go into the forest, or to live in communes. Because there comes a point when they get so fed up with existing social structures that they want to run away to find their salvation—and salvation invariably means living closer to Nature. Now, it would be a mistake to assume that Shakespeare thought this was a marvellous, joyful thing to do. When it came to the solutions which, because they are human solutions, are necessarily imperfect, he had to say, "It is marvellous to run away, to live in the midst of Nature, but don't believe for a single second that living in the midst of Nature does not involve the same kind of politics – power politics – and exploitation that exist when you live in the city. Except the poor beasts can't talk back. That's all." The dialogue about which is the better way for men to live in a civilized fashion—either in the court or in the forest—is an ongoing discussion which is at the very basis of Western literature, culture, society. You will find the Romans having the same dialogue the Elizabethans had and, indeed, as the Woodstock people had.

In the midst of the play, there is a kind of dance for a quartet of lovers. What is that all about? It concerns the necessity of "coupling," of continuity, of carrying on life whether you live in the city or in the forest. In short, there is a very important and, for me, a very profound statement. You can talk and talk about whether it's better to live here or there, but finally, when it gets down to brass tacks, there have to be weddings. If there are no weddings, there are no children. And if there are no children, there can be no discussion about whether to live here or there. The dance consists of this crazy analysis of how people are attracted to one another and why. Most loving is mere folly. Shakespeare realizes that all his romancing is really Nature's way of capturing people – couples – to procreate. And there is some kind of a great metaphysical mating dance in the shape of these romances wherein they are blinded; their emotions and their glands are working a mile a minute; and they get caught in the Venus's fly-trap – except that it's Nature who is Venus's fly-trap. And it is essential that the people who are engaged in this search for partners be blind or half-blind; otherwise the thing doesn't work. It is essential that illusion be at the centre of romantic love. The partners do not see one another the way they really are. We are all creatures with the ideal film image in our heads, forever looking for the ideal silver screen of a person on whom we can project our ideas – for a while, at any rate. And we rerun the film over and over again as long as we find the same screen. We can't break it. All the people who keep on divorcing and remarrying keep remarrying the same types over and over again. Nobody learns. Or those who do are very lucky and they are one in ten million. I haven't met too many people like that.

So, who are these people in *As You Like It*? Rosalind is a lady who knows romantic love is an illusion. She can't stand the idea that she has no control over these foolish things that go on. She is in love, and she knows exactly what is happening to her, but she can't help it. She is, in effect, the most conscious of these crazy, drunken lovers who are dancing around in the middle of the forest.

Celia obviously doesn't think that she'll ever find anyone who will love her, but underneath, her film is running twenty times a day. It is more romantic and more passionate, fancier and richer, than anybody else's. And this is why, when Oliver appears, they fall in love in minutes. And that can only be possible – if you're logical about this – if everything is already there in their heads. Love at first sight: What does it mean? Finally you've found the perfect cast, the perfect set, the perfect costumes for your play. But the play is in the head and that's what we have to remember.

Orlando, as a lover, is tremendously attracted to bright women. Now, he senses that he is dealing with someone, in the person of Rosalind/Ganymede, who is extraordinarily intelligent, imaginative, attractive, capable of romance. Orlando and Rosalind are very, very much in tune. She is brighter than he is, but he has extraordinarily well-developed moral qualities. In the Rosalind/Orlando relationship, there is a lot of talk, this oral eroticism, I call it. In this play you go through many brilliant passages of conversation, but there is something incredibly erotic about all this talking. It is the most convoluted language that you can imagine, which is nothing more than a disguise for sexual feelings and conflict.

In contrast, the shepherdess Phebe is closer to Nature. Yet she, too, dreams of this prince on a white charger and this bumpkin Silvius will not fill the bill. Meanwhile, he cannot feel, cannot think of anything or anyone but her. He is Romeo roaming the forest aflame with passion, bumping into trees, howling at the moon, rolling on the floor of the forest, stockings undone, garlands in his hair: "I'll take romance"—he believes every word of it, but he feels hopeless, absolutely hopeless, because Phebe is infatuated with this youth, Ganymede, whom she sees according to her own film.

And then come Touchstone and Audrey – and we hit rock bottom there. Touchstone is a pure and absolutely dirty old man – he goes for big girls, and they've got to be slightly ripe! For him, there is nothing there but pure and absolute sex, and that is what he finds in the forest. That's his Arden, his Eden. As far as Audrey is concerned, she is totally innocent; her sexuality is totally unself-conscious. It is just there. She adores attention, like every human being, and Touchstone gives her the kind of attention she has never had. He is funny. He sings songs. He pulls handkerchiefs out of her ear. He comes from the city. Of course, he's a randy old goat, but who cares? She's never seen anything like him.

The person who doesn't have a partner in all this crazy dance is Jaques. He is the archetypal loner, the person who suffers from some kind of deep wound that turns him against the world. Nobody can be turned against the world with a kind of cynicism who has not been hurt by the world and who is not incredibly sensitive. I keep seeing him weeping for no reason whatsoever. He sits under a tree and weeps. The magic doesn't work for him. The film that runs in his head has never found its silver screen.

If intellect and imagination are well balanced in Orlando, and if Silvius is carrying on in a Romeo-like way, and if Touchstone is raw sexuality, William is the most innocent and the most inarticulate of lovers. He has none of the weapons, none of the artifices with which to woo Audrey. He is dispossessed by the arrival in the forest of all these city slickers who think that they are liberated. He follows Audrey around all the time, peeking out from behind trees. But he is not a tragic figure, someone who is to be pitied. He loses out – but one can imagine that in two months she will be back.

Oliver and Frederick: There is a school of criticism about the romances that claims their conversions are unbelievable. But none of these people took into account the first point that I made: This is a fairy tale. If a frog can turn into a prince, an evil duke can turn into a "convertite." I've seen a lot of frogs turn into princes and a lot of princes turn into frogs. It is the same with Oliver: Because it is a fairy tale, it is entirely proper and possible that, through some magic, through some revelation, people do change.

None of this works if one misunderstands what I am talking about –

namely, that these fairy tales are peopled with one-dimensional cartoon characters. They come alive only if you are able to take these incredibly rich archetypes and bring your own experiences to them. Being in this play gives you a marvellous opportunity to discover the nature of your own loving.

Now, let me just tell you what I see happening on the stage at the very beginning of *As You Like It*. Because we are talking about a play of transformation – a transformation of souls from evil to good, transformation of Nature going from Winter to Spring, darkness to light in this production – the play opens in a village – it is really Oliver's village – and when the lights come up (and there are very, very few lights that do come up) you see the winter streets covered with snow. It is very cold. There is a little boy, very scantily attired, on a chain that is held by a man playing a hurdy-gurdy. There are people huddled on the stage. The boy is singing "Under the Greenwood Tree" in a reedy, little broken voice. People cross the stage with wood and a brace of freshly killed rabbits; there are two soldiers leading a man toward what could be an execution. His arms are tied; he's without shoes in the snow. The boy sings on. The music goes on. And you are in the middle of darkness, winter, and poverty and death and impending danger. And then, when the people have crossed, Orlando and Adam come on, and the play begins.

John S Hirsch

Andrew Gillies as Orlando

A Note to the Reader

The text used in the 1983 Stratford Festival Edition of *As You Like It* is based on the Globe Text, with references to the First Folio. It incorporates generally accepted modern spellings and punctuation.

A glossary of Elizabethan and unfamiliar terms appears at the bottom of the pages.

The Act and Scene numbers are given at the top of each right-hand page. The Scene numbers enclosed in brackets in the right-hand margin indicate the way the play was divided for rehearsal purposes at Stratford. During a performance the stage manager uses these Scene numbers to call cues for lights, sound, and orchestra.

Also in the right-hand margin is the over-all numerical delineation; the Stratford Festival Edition delineation is enclosed in brackets. The SF line numbers refer the reader to a set of emendations at the end of the text. These emendations include word changes, line changes, cuts, and additions that were made specifically for the 1983 Stratford Festival Production of *As You Like It*. Also included are paraphrases of particularly difficult lines.

The 1983 Stratford Festival Production of

As You Like It

Directed by John Hirsch
Designed by Desmond Heeley
Music by Raymond Pannell
Lighting designed by Michael J. Whitefield
Choreography by John Broome

The Cast

Orlando } sons of Sir Rowland de Boys		Andrew Gillies
Oliver		Stephen Russell
Adam } servants to Oliver		Mervyn Blake
Dennis		Nicolas Colicos
Charles, wrestler to Duke Frederick		Jefferson Mappin
Rosalind, daughter to the Duke Senior		Roberta Maxwell
Celia, daughter to Duke Frederick		Rosemary Dunsmore
Touchstone, a clown		Lewis Gordon
Le Beau, a courtier to Duke Frederick		Keith Dinicol
Duke Frederick, the Duke Senior's brother and usurper of his dominions		Graeme Campbell

First Frederick Lord	Steve Yorke
Second Frederick Lord	Peter Zednik
Duke Senior, living in banishment	William Needles
Amiens, lord attending on the Duke Senior	John Novak
First Forest Lord	Thomas Hauff
Second Forest Lord	Michael Shepherd
Silvius ⎱ shepherds	John Jarvis
Corin ⎰	Deryck Hazel
Jaques, lord attending on the Duke Senior	Nicholas Pennell
Audrey, a country wench	Elizabeth Leigh-Milne
Sir Oliver Martext, a vicar	Maurice E. Evans
Phebe, a shepherdess	Mary Haney
William, a country fellow in love with Audrey	Hardee T. Lineham
First Page	Christopher Cook
Second Page	Graham Abbey
Jaques de Boys	Robert Lachance

Townspeople, Courtiers, Soldiers, and Forest Lords:
Graham Abbey, Simon Bradbury, Paddy Campanaro, Nicolas Colicos, Christopher Cook, Holly Dennison, Simon du Toit, Maurice E. Evans, Christopher Gibson, Thomas Hauff, Robert Lachance, Greg Lawson, Jefferson Mappin, Michael McKeever, Seana McKenna, John Novak, Elizabeth Rukavina, Ric Sarabia, John Shafer, Michael Shepherd, David Smith, Marie Stillin, Patrick Tierney, Christiane Vaillancourt, E. Joan Warren, Tim Whelan, Jan Wood, Steve Yorke, Peter Zednik

Assistant Director:	Don Bouzek
Stage Manager:	Michael Shamata
Assistant Stage Managers:	Victoria Klein and Jill Orenstein
Assistant Designer:	Polly Scranton Bohdanetzky
Assistant Lighting Designer:	Peter McKinnon
Movement and Fight Director:	John Broome

Stephen Russell as Oliver, Mervyn Blake as Adam, and Andrew Gillies

Act First

Scene 1

Orchard of Oliver's house
Enter Orlando and Adam

Orlando As I remember, Adam, it was upon this fashion
bequeathed me by will, but poor a thousand crowns,   [2]
and, as thou sayest, charged my brother, on his
blessing, to breed me well: and there begins my
sadness. My brother Jaques he keeps at school, and
report speaks goldenly of his profit. For my part,
he keeps me rustically at home, or, to speak more
properly, stays me here at home unkept; for call
you that keeping for a gentleman of my birth, that
differs not from the stalling of an ox? His horses   10
are bred better, for, besides that they are fair with   [11-13]
their feeding, they are taught their manage, and to
that end riders dearly hired: but I, his brother, gain
nothing under him but growth, for the which his
animals on his dunghills are as much bound to him
as I. Besides this nothing that he so plentifully
gives me, the something that nature gave me his
countenance seems to take from me. He lets me
feed with his hinds, bars me the place of a brother,
and, as much as in him lies, mines my gentility with   [20]
my education. This is it, Adam, that grieves me,   [21]
and the spirit of my father, which I think is within
me, begins to mutiny against this servitude. I will

---

  2 Line numbers in brackets refer to Emendations,
     pp. 118-133. See also Note, p. 7.
  5 **school:** university
 19 **hinds:** menials

	no longer endure it, though yet I know no wise
	remedy how to avoid it.
Adam	Yonder comes my master, your brother.
Orlando	Go apart, Adam, and thou shalt hear how he will
	shake me up.

Enter Oliver

Oliver	Now, sir! What make you here?	
Orlando	Nothing. I am not taught to make any thing.	30
Oliver	What mar you then, sir?	
Orlando	Marry, sir, I am helping you to mar that which God	
	made, a poor unworthy brother of yours, with	
	idleness.	
Oliver	Marry, sir, be better employed, and be naught awhile.	[35]
Orlando	Shall I keep your hogs, and eat husks with them?	
	What prodigal portion have I spent, that I should	
	come to such penury?	
Oliver	Know you where you are, sir?	
Orlando	O, sir, very well; here in your orchard.	40
Oliver	Know you before whom, sir?	
Orlando	Ay, better than him I am before knows me. I know	
	you are my eldest brother, and in the gentle con-	
	dition of blood you should so know me. The	
	courtesy of nations allows you my better, in that you	
	are the first-born, but the same tradition takes not	
	away my blood, were there twenty brothers betwixt	
	us. I have as much of my father in me as you, albeit	[48-50]
	I confess your coming before me is nearer to his	
	reverence.	50
Oliver	What, boy!	
Orlando	Come, come, elder brother, you are too young in	[52-53]
	this.	
Oliver	Wilt thou lay hands on me, villain?	
Orlando	I am no villain; I am the youngest son of Sir	
	Rowland de Boys; he was my father, and he is	
	thrice a villain that says such a father begot villains.	
	Wert thou not my brother, I would not take this	[58-62]
	hand from thy throat till this other had pulled out	
	thy tongue for saying so: thou hast railed on thyself.	60
Adam	Sweet masters, be patient: for your father's re-	
	membrance, be at accord.	

---

37 **prodigal:** wasteful, extravagant

Oliver	Let me go, I say.	[63]
Orlando	I will not, till I please: you shall hear me. My father charged you in his will to give me good education: you have trained me like a peasant, obscuring and hiding from me all gentlemanlike qualities. The spirit of my father grows strong in me, and I will no longer endure it: therefore allow me such exercises as may become a gentleman, or give me the poor allottery my father left me by testament; with that I will go buy my fortunes.	70
Oliver	And what wilt thou do? Beg, when that is spent? Well, sir, get you in. I will not long be troubled with you; you shall have some part of your will. I pray you, leave me.	
Orlando	I will no further offend you than becomes me for my good.	
Oliver	Get you with him, you old dog.	
Adam	Is 'old dog' my reward? Most true, I have lost my teeth in your service. God be with my old master! He would not have spoke such a word.	80
	Exeunt Orlando and Adam	[Scene 2]
Oliver	Is it even so? Begin you to grow upon me? I will physic your rankness, and yet give no thousand crowns neither. Holla, Dennis!	[84] [85]

Enter Dennis

Dennis	Calls your worship?	
Oliver	Was not Charles, the Duke's wrestler, here to speak with me?	
Dennis	So please you, he is here at the door, and importunes access to you.	[89-90] 90
Oliver	Call him in. *(Exit Dennis.)* 'Twill be a good way; and to-morrow the wrestling is.	[91]

Enter Charles

Charles	Good morrow to your worship.
Oliver	Good Monsieur Charles, what's the new news at the new court?
Charles	There's no news at the court, sir, but the old news: that is, the old Duke is banished by his younger brother the new Duke; and three or four loving

---

71 **allottery:** inheritance

	lords have put themselves into voluntary exile with	
	him, whose lands and revenues enrich the new Duke;	100
	therefore he gives them good leave to wander.	
Oliver	Can you tell if Rosalind, the Duke's daughter,	
	be banished with her father?	
Charles	O, no; for the Duke's daughter, her cousin, so	[104-07]
	loves her, being ever from their cradles bred together,	
	that she would have followed her exile, or have died	
	to stay behind her. She is at the court, and no less	
	beloved of her uncle than his own daughter; and	
	never two ladies loved as they do.	
Oliver	Where will the old Duke live?	110
Charles	They say he is already in the Forest of Arden, and	
	a many merry men with him; and there they live	
	like the old Robin Hood of England: they say many	[113-114]
	young gentlemen flock to him every day, and fleet	
	the time carelessly as they did in the golden world.	
Oliver	What, you wrestle to-morrow before the new Duke?	
Charles	Marry, do I, sir; and I came to acquaint you with	
	a matter. I am given, sir, secretly to understand	
	that your younger brother, Orlando, hath a disposi-	
	tion to come in disguised against me to try a fall.	120
	To-morrow, sir, I wrestle for my credit, and he that	
	escapes me without some broken limb shall acquit	
	him well. Your brother is but young and tender,	
	and for your love I would be loath to foil him, as	[124-25]
	I must for my own honour if he come in. Therefore,	
	out of my love to you, I came hither to acquaint you	
	withal, that either you might stay him from his	
	intendment, or brook such disgrace well as he shall	[128]
	run into, in that it is a thing of his own search, and	[129-30]
	altogether against my will.	130
Oliver	Charles, I thank thee for thy love to me, which thou	
	shalt find I will most kindly requite. I had myself	
	taken notice of my brother's purpose herein, and have by	
	underhand means laboured to dissuade him from it;	
	but he is resolute. I'll tell thee, Charles, it is the	
	stubbornest young fellow of France, full of ambition,	
	an envious emulator of every man's good parts, a	

---

115 **golden world:** Golden Age
124 **foil:** defeat

secret and villanous contriver against me his natural
brother. Therefore use thy discretion; I had as lief
thou didst break his neck as his finger. And thou   140
wert best look to 't; for if thou dost him any slight
disgrace, or if he do not mightily grace himself on
thee, he will practice against thee by poison, entrap
thee by some treacherous device, and never leave
thee till he hath ta'en thy life by some indirect means
or other; for I assure thee, and almost with tears   [146-50]
I speak it, there is not one so young and so villanous
this day living. I speak but brotherly of him; but
should I anatomize him to thee, as he is, I must blush,
and weep, and thou must look pale and wonder.   150

Charles   I am heartily glad I came hither to you. If he come
to-morrow, I'll give him his payment: if ever he go
alone again, I'll never wrestle for prize more. And
so, God keep your worship!

Oliver   Farewell, good Charles. *(Exit Charles.)* Now will I
stir this gamester. I hope I shall see an end of him;
for my soul, yet I know not why, hates nothing
more than he. Yet he's gentle, never schooled, and
yet learned, full of noble device, of all sorts enchant-
ingly beloved, and indeed so much in the heart of   160
the world, and especially of my own people, who
best know him, that I am altogether misprised. But
it shall not be so long, this wrestler shall clear all.
Nothing remains but that I kindle the boy thither,   [164-65]
which now I'll go about.   *Exit*

---

139 **had as lief:** would as willingly
149 **anatomize:** analyze minutely
153 **go alone:** walk without support
162 **am ... misprised:** misunderstood

Scene 2 [Scene 3]

Lawn before the Duke's palace
Enter Rosalind and Celia

Celia	I pray thee, Rosalind, sweet my coz, be merry.
Rosalind	Dear Celia, I show more mirth than I am mistress of, and would you yet I were merrier? Unless you could teach me to forget a banished father, you must not learn me how to remember any extraordinary pleasure.
Celia	Herein I see thou lovest me not with the full weight that I love thee. If my uncle, thy banished father, had banished thy uncle, the Duke my father, so thou hadst been still with me, I could have taught my love 10 to take thy father for mine: so wouldst thou, if the truth of thy love to me were so righteously tempered as mine is to thee.
Rosalind	Well, I will forget the condition of my estate, to rejoice in yours.
Celia	You know my father hath no child but I, nor none is like to have; and, truly, when he dies, thou shalt be his heir; for what he hath taken away from thy father perforce, I will render thee again in affection; by mine honour, I will, and when I break that oath, 20 let me turn monster. Therefore, my sweet Rose, my dear Rose, be merry.
Rosalind	From henceforth I will, coz, and devise sports. Let me see; what think you of falling in love?
Celia	Marry, I prithee, do, to make sport withal: but love no man in good earnest, nor no further in sport neither, than with safety of a pure blush thou mayst in honour come off again.
Rosalind	What shall be our sport, then?
Celia	Let us sit and mock the good housewife Fortune from [30] her wheel, that her gifts may henceforth be bestowed equally.
Rosalind	I would we could do so; for her benefits are mightily misplaced, and the bountiful blind woman doth most mistake in her gifts to women.

1	**coz:** cousin	**Rosemary Dunsmore**
5	**learn:** teach	**as Celia and Roberta Maxwell**
19	**perforce:** forcibly	**as Rosalind▶**

Celia	'Tis true, for those that she makes fair she scarce makes honest, and those that she makes honest she makes very ill-favouredly.
Rosalind	Nay, now thou goest from Fortune's office to Nature's: Fortune reigns in gifts of the world, not in the lineaments of Nature. [40]

Enter Touchstone

Celia	No? When Nature hath made a fair creature, may she not by Fortune fall into the fire? Though Nature hath given us wit to flout at Fortune, hath not Fortune sent in this fool to cut off the argument?
Rosalind	Indeed, there is Fortune too hard for Nature, when [46-53] Fortune makes Nature's natural the cutter-off of Nature's wit.
Celia	Peradventure this is not Fortune's work neither, but Nature's; who perceiveth our natural wits too dull 50 to reason of such goddesses, hath sent this natural for our whetstone; for always the dulness of the fool is the whetstone of the wits. How now, wit, whither wander you?
Touchstone	Mistress, you must come away to your father.
Celia	Were you made the messenger?
Touchstone	No, by mine honour, but I was bid to come for you.
Rosalind	Where learned you that oath, fool? [58]
Touchstone	Of a certain knight, that swore by his honour they were good pancakes, and swore by his honour [60] the mustard was naught; now I'll stand to it, the pancakes were naught, and the mustard was good, [62] and yet was not the knight forsworn.
Celia	How prove you that in the great heap of your knowledge?
Rosalind	Ay, marry, now unmuzzle your wisdom.
Touchstone	Stand you both forth now: stroke your chins, and swear by your beards that I am a knave.
Celia	By our beards, if we had them, thou art.
Touchstone	By my knavery, if I had it, then I were; but if 70 you swear by that that is not, you are not forsworn: no more was this knight swearing by his honour, for

41 **lineaments:** (facial) features
44 **flout:** mock
52 **whetstone:** stone used to give a smooth edge to cutting tools

	he never had any; or if he had, he had sworn it	
	away, before ever he saw those pancakes, or that	[74]
	mustard.	
Celia	Prithee, who is't that thou meanest?	
Touchstone	One that old Frederick, your father, loves.	
Celia	My father's love is enough to honour him: enough!	[78-80]
	speak no more of him; you'll be whipped for taxa-	
	tion one of these days.	80
Touchstone	The more pity, that fools may not speak wisely	
	what wise men do foolishly.	
Celia	By my troth, thou sayest true; for since the little	
	wit that fools have was silenced, the little foolery	
	that wise men have makes a great show. Here	
	comes Monsieur the Beu.	[86]
Rosalind	With his mouth full of news.	
Celia	Which he will put on us, as pigeons feed their young.	
Rosalind	Then shall we be news-crammed.	
Celia	All the better; we shall be the more marketable.	90

Enter Le Beau

	Bon jour, Monsieur Le Beau; what's the news?	
Le Beau	Fair princess, you have lost much good sport.	
Celia	Sport! Of what colour?	
Le Beau	What colour, madam! How shall I answer you?	
Rosalind	As wit and fortune will.	
Touchstone	Or as the Destinies decrees.	
Celia	Well said: that was laid on with a trowel.	
Touchstone	Nay, if I keep not my rank, –	
Rosalind	Thou losest thy old smell.	[99]
Le Beau	You amaze me, ladies: I would have told you	100
	of good wrestling, which you have lost the sight	
	of.	
Rosalind	Yet tell us the manner of the wrestling.	
Le Beau	I will tell you the beginning; and, if it please	
	your ladyships, you may see the end, for the best is	
	yet to do, and here, where you are, they are coming	
	to perform it.	
Celia	Well, the beginning that is dead and buried.	

---

93 **colour:** type

LE BEAU.

Le Beau	There comes an old man and his three sons, –	
Celia	I could match this beginning with an old tale.	110
Le Beau	Three proper young men, of excellent growth and presence.	
Rosalind	With bills on their necks, 'Be it known unto all men by these presents.'	[113-14]
Le Beau	The eldest of the three wrestled with Charles, the Duke's wrestler, which Charles in a moment threw him, and broke three of his ribs, that there is little hope of life in him: so he served the second, and so the third. Yonder they lie, the poor old man, their father, making such pitiful dole over them that all the beholders take his part with weeping.	120
Rosalind	Alas!	
Touchstone	But what is the sport, monsieur, that the ladies have lost?	
Le Beau	Why, this that I speak of.	
Touchstone	Thus men may grow wiser every day: it is the first time that ever I heard breaking of ribs was sport for ladies.	
Celia	Or I, I promise thee.	130
Rosalind	But is there any else longs to see this broken music in his sides? Is there yet another dotes upon rib-breaking? Shall we see this wrestling, cousin?	
Le Beau	You must if you stay here, for here is the place appointed for the wrestling, and they are ready to perform it.	
Celia	Yonder, sure, they are coming: let us now stay and see it.	

Flourish. Enter Duke Frederick, Lords, Orlando,   [Scene 4]
Charles, and Attendants

Frederick	Come on: since the youth will not be entreated, his own peril on his forwardness.	140
Rosalind	Is yonder the man?	
Le Beau	Even he, madam.	
Celia	Alas, he is too young! Yet he looks successfully.	
Frederick	How now, daughter, and cousin; are you crept	

---

120 **dole**: mourning

21

	hither to see the wrestling?	
Rosalind	Ay, my liege, so please you give us leave.	
Frederick	You will take little delight in it, I can tell you,	
	there is such odds in the man. In pity of the chal-	
	lenger's youth I would fain dissuade him, but he	
	will not be entreated. Speak to him, ladies, see if	150
	you can move him.	
Celia	Call him hither, good Monsieur Le Beau.	
Frederick	Do so: I'll not be by.	
Le Beau	Monsieur the challenger, the princess calls for you.	
Orlando	I attend them with all respect and duty.	
Rosalind	Young man, have you challenged Charles the	
	wrestler?	
Orlando	No, fair princess; he is the general challenger: I	
	come but in as others do, to try with him the strength	
	of my youth.	160
Celia	Young gentleman, your spirits are too bold for your	
	years. You have seen cruel proof of this man's	
	strength: if you saw yourself with your eyes, or	
	knew yourself with your judgement, the fear of your	
	adventure would counsel you to a more equal enter-	
	prise. We pray you for your own sake to embrace	
	your own safety, and give over this attempt.	
Rosalind	Do, young sir; your reputation shall not therefore	
	be misprised: we will make it our suit to the Duke	
	that the wrestling might not go forward.	170
Orlando	I beseech you, punish me not with your hard	
	thoughts, wherein I confess me much guilty to deny	
	so fair and excellent ladies any thing. But let your	
	fair eyes and gentle wishes go with me to my trial:	
	wherein if I be foiled, there is but one shamed that	
	was never gracious; if killed, but one dead that is	
	willing to be so: I shall do my friends no wrong,	
	for I have none to lament me; the world no injury,	
	for in it I have nothing: only in the world I fill up	
	a place, which may be better supplied, when I have	180
	made it empty.	
Rosalind	The little strength that I have, I would it were with	
	you.	

149 **fain:** willingly

Celia	And mine to eke out hers.
Rosalind	Fare you well: pray heaven I be deceived in you!
Celia	Your heart's desires be with you!
Charles	Come, where is this young gallant that is so desirous to lie with his mother earth?
Orlando	Ready, sir; but his will hath in it a more modest working.
Frederick	You shall try but one fall.
Charles	No, I warrant your Grace you shall not entreat him to a second, that have so mightily persuaded him from a first.
Orlando	You mean to mock me after; you should not have mocked me before: but come your ways.
Rosalind	Now Hercules be thy speed, young man!
Celia	I would I were invisible, to catch the strong fellow by the leg. *They wrestle*
Rosalind	O excellent young man!
Celia	If I had a thunderbolt in mine eye, I can tell who should down. *Shout. Charles is thrown*
Frederick	No more, no more.
Orlando	Yes, I beseech your Grace, I am not yet well breath'd.
Frederick	How dost thou, Charles?
Le Beau	He cannot speak, my lord.
Frederick	Bear him away. What is thy name, young man?
Orlando	Orlando, my liege, the youngest son of Sir Rowland de Boys.
Frederick	I would thou hadst been son to some man else: The world esteem'd thy father honourable, But I did find him still mine enemy. Thou shouldst have better pleas'd me with this deed, Hadst thou descended from another house. But fair thee well, thou art a gallant youth; I would thou hadst told me of another father.

Exeunt Duke Frederick, train, and Le Beau   [Scene 5]

Celia	Were I my father, coz, would I do this?
Orlando	I am more proud to be Sir Rowland's son, His youngest son, and would not change that calling To be adopted heir to Frederick.

190

200

210

220

Orlando and Charles, played by Jefferson Mappin, in the wrestling scene.

Rosalind	My father lov'd Sir Rowland as his soul,
	And all the world was of my father's mind:
	Had I before known this young man his son,
	I should have given him tears unto entreaties,
	Ere he should thus have ventur'd.
Celia	Gentle cousin,
	Let us go thank him, and encourage him:
	My father's rough and envious disposition
	Sticks me at heart. Sir, you have well deserv'd:
	If you do keep your promises in love,
	But justly as you have exceeded all promise,
	Your mistress shall be happy.
Rosalind	Gentleman,

Giving him a chain from her neck

	Wear this for me; one out of suits with fortune,
	That could give more, but that her hand lacks means.
	Shall we go, coz?
Celia	Ay. Fare you well, fair gentleman.
Orlando	Can I not say, I thank you? My better parts
	Are all thrown down, and that which here stands up
	Is but a quintain, a mere lifeless block.
Rosalind	He calls us back. My pride fell with my fortunes;
	I'll ask him what he would. Did you call, sir?
	Sir, you have wrestled well, and overthrown
	More than your enemies.
Celia	Will you go, coz?
Rosalind	Have with you: fare you well.

Exeunt Rosalind and Celia

Orlando	What passion hangs these weights upon my tongue?
	I cannot speak to her, yet she urged conference.
	O poor Orlando, thou art overthrown!
	Or Charles, or something weaker, masters thee.

Re-enter Le Beau   [Scene 6]

Le Beau	Good sir, I do in friendship counsel you
	To leave this place. Albeit you have deserv'd
	High commendation, true applause, and love,
	Yet such is now the Duke's condition,
	That he misconsters all that you have done.

---

232 **out of suits:** out of favour
237 **quintain:** block or figure used for tilting practice
251 **misconsters:** misconstrues

	The Duke is humorous; what he is, indeed,	
	More suits you to conceive than I to speak of.	
Orlando	I thank you, sir: and pray you tell me this,	
	Which of the two was daughter of the Duke,	
	That here was at the wrestling?	
Le Beau	Neither his daughter, if we judge by manners,	
	But yet, indeed, the taller is his daughter;	[258]
	The other is daughter to the banish'd Duke,	
	And here detain'd by her usurping uncle	260
	To keep his daughter company, whose loves	
	Are dearer than the natural bond of sisters.	
	But I can tell you that of late this Duke	
	Hath ta'en displeasure 'gainst his gentle niece,	
	Grounded upon no other argument	
	But that the people praise her for her virtues,	
	And pity her, for her good father's sake;	
	And, on my life, his malice 'gainst the lady	
	Will suddenly break forth. Sir, fare you well;	
	Hereafter in a better world than this,	270
	I shall desire more love and knowledge of you.	
Orlando	I rest much bounden to you: fare you well.	

Exit Le Beau

Thus must I from the smoke into the smother,
From tyrant Duke, unto a tyrant brother:
But heavenly Rosalind!   *Exit*

---

252 **humorous:** moody
273 **smother:** dense smoke

Scene 3

A room in the palace
Enter Celia and Rosalind

Celia	Why, cousin! Why, Rosalind! Cupid have mercy! Not a word?	
Rosalind	Not one to throw at a dog.	
Celia	No, thy words are too precious to be cast away upon curs; throw some of them at me; come lame me with reasons.	
Rosalind	Then there were two cousins laid up, when the one should be lamed with reasons, and the other mad without any.	
Celia	But is all this for your father?	10
Rosalind	No, some of it is for my child's father. O, how full of briers is this working-day world!	
Celia	They are but burs, cousin, thrown upon thee in holiday foolery; if we walk not in the trodden paths, our very petticoats will catch them.	
Rosalind	I could shake them off my coat; these burs are in my heart.	
Celia	Hem them away.	
Rosalind	I would try if I could cry hem, and have him.	
Celia	Come, come, wrestle with thy affections.	20
Rosalind	O, they take the part of a better wrestler than myself!	
Celia	O, a good wish upon you! You will try in time, in despite of a fall. But, turning these jests out of service, let us talk in good earnest. Is it possible, on such a sudden, you should fall into so strong a liking with old Sir Rowland's youngest son?	[22-24]
Rosalind	The Duke my father loved his father dearly.	
Celia	Doth it therefore ensue that you should love his son dearly? By this kind of chase, I should hate him, for my father hated his father dearly; yet I hate not Orlando.	30
Rosalind	No, faith, hate him not, for my sake.	
Celia	Why should I not? Doth he not deserve well?	
Rosalind	Let me love him for that, and do you love him because I do. Look, here comes the Duke.	[35-36]

---

18 **Hem:** a cough to clear the throat

Celia	With his eyes full of anger.

Enter Duke Frederick, with Lords

Frederick	Mistress, dispatch you with your safest haste,
	And get you from our court.
Rosalind	Me, uncle?
Frederick	You, cousin,
	Within these ten days if that thou be'st found
	So near our public court as twenty miles, 40
	Thou diest for it.
Rosalind	I do beseech your Grace,
	Let me the knowledge of my fault bear with me:
	If with myself I hold intelligence,
	Or have acquaintance with mine own desires,
	If that I do not dream, or be not frantic, – [45-46]
	As I do trust I am not, – then, dear uncle,
	Never so much as in a thought unborn
	Did I offend your Highness.
Frederick	Thus do all traitors:
	If their purgation did consist in words,
	They are as innocent as grace itself. 50
	Let it suffice thee that I trust thee not.
Rosalind	Yet your mistrust cannot make me a traitor:
	Tell me whereon the likelihood depends.
Frederick	Thou art thy father's daughter, there's enough.
Rosalind	So was I when your Highness took his dukedom,
	So was I when your Highness banish'd him.
	Treason is not inherited, my lord,
	Or, if we did derive it from our friends,
	What's that to me? My father was no traitor.
	Then, good my liege, mistake me not so much 60
	To think my poverty is treacherous.
Celia	Dear sovereign, hear me speak.
Frederick	Ay, Celia; we stay'd her for your sake,
	Else had she with her father rang'd along.
Celia	I did not then entreat to have her stay,
	It was your pleasure, and your own remorse;
	I was too young that time to value her,
	But now I know her: if she be a traitor,

---

45 **frantic:** mad
63 **stay'd her:** let her stay

The banishment scene: Duke Frederick (center), played by
Graeme Campbell, and his Lords, with Celia and Rosalind

	Why so am I; we still have slept together,
	Rose at an instant, learn'd, play'd, ate together,	70
	And wheresoe'er we went, like Juno's swans,	[71]
	Still we went coupled and inseparable.
Frederick	She is too subtle for thee, and her smoothness,
	Her very silence, and her patience,
	Speak to the people, and they pity her.
	Thou art a fool, she robs thee of thy name,
	And thou wilt show more bright, and seem more
	virtuous,
	When she is gone. Then open not thy lips:
	Firm and irrevocable is my doom,
	Which I have pass'd upon her; she is banish'd.	80
Celia	Pronounce that sentence then on me, my liege;
	I cannot live out of her company.
Frederick	You are a fool. You, niece, provide yourself;
	If you outstay the time, upon mine honour,
	And in the greatness of my word, you die.

Exeunt Duke Frederick and Lords

Celia	O my poor Rosalind, whither wilt thou go?
	Wilt thou change fathers? I will give thee mine.
	I charge thee, be not thou more griev'd than I am.
Rosalind	I have more cause.
Celia	Thou hast not, cousin.
	Prithee, be cheerful: know'st thou not the Duke	90
	Hath banish'd me, his daughter?
Rosalind	That he hath not.
Celia	No, hath not? Rosalind lacks then the love
	Which teacheth thee that thou and I am one.
	Shall we be sunder'd? Shall we part, sweet girl?
	No, let my father seek another heir.
	Therefore devise with me how we may fly,
	Whither to go, and what to bear with us,
	And do not seek to take your change upon you,
	To bear your griefs yourself, and leave me out;

	For by this heaven, now at our sorrows pale,	100
	Say what thou canst, I'll go along with thee.	
Rosalind	Why, whither shall we go?	
Celia	To seek my uncle in the Forest of Arden.	
Rosalind	Alas, what danger will it be to us,	

Maids as we are, to travel forth so far?
Beauty provoketh thieves sooner than gold.

Celia
I'll put myself in poor and mean attire,
And with a kind of umber smirch my face;
The like do you: so shall we pass along,
And never stir assailants.

Rosalind   Were it not better,   110
Because that I am more than common tall,   [111]
That I did suit me all points like a man,
A gallant curtle-axe upon my thigh,
A boar-spear in my hand? And – in my heart
Lie there what hidden woman's fear there will –
We'll have a swashing and a martial outside,
As many other mannish cowards have,
That do outface it with their semblances.

Celia
What shall I call thee when thou art a man?

Rosalind
I'll have no worse a name than Jove's own page,   120
And therefore look you call me Ganymede.
But what will you be call'd?

Celia
Something that hath a reference to my state:
No longer Celia, but Aliena.

Rosalind
But, cousin, what if we assay'd to steal
The clownish fool out of your father's court?
Would he not be a comfort to our travel?

Celia
He'll go along o'er the wide world with me;
Leave me alone to woo him. Let's away,
And get our jewels and our wealth together,   130
Devise the fittest time, and safest way
To hide us from pursuit that will be made
After my flight. Now go we in content
To liberty, and not to banishment.   *Exeunt*

---

108 **umber:** brownish earth
   smirch: discolour
113 **curtle-axe:** cutlass
116 **swashing:** swaggering, swashbuckling
118 **outface it:** bluff it out
121 **Ganymede:** (Myth.) a youth who was abducted
   and made cupbearer of the gods and became immortal
125 **assay'd:** endeavoured

John Novak as Amiens

Act Second

Scene

The Forest of Arden
Enter Duke Senior, Amiens, and two or three Lords, like
foresters

Duke Senior	Now, my co-mates, and brothers in exile,
	Hath not old custom made this life more sweet
	Than that of painted pomp? Are not these woods
	More free from peril than the envious court?
	Here feel we not the penalty of Adam,
	The seasons' difference, as the icy fang
	And churlish chiding of the winter's wind,
	Which, when it bites and blows upon my body,
	Even till I shrink with cold, I smile, and say
	'This is no flattery: these are counsellors
	That feelingly persuade me what I am.'
	Sweet are the uses of adversity,
	Which, like the toad, ugly and venomous,
	Wears yet a precious jewel in his head.
	And this our life, exempt from public haunt,
	Finds tongues in trees, books in the running brooks,
	Sermons in stones, and good in every thing.
	I would not change it.
Amiens	Happy is your Grace,
	That can translate the stubbornness of fortune
	Into so quiet and so sweet a style.
Duke Senior	Come, shall we go and kill us venison?
	And yet it irks me the poor dappled fools,

Line numbers: 10, [13-14], 20

22 **fools:** simple creatures

	Being native burghers of this desert city,	
	Should in their own confines with forked heads	
	Have their round haunches gored.	
First Lord	Indeed, my lord,	
	The melancholy Jaques grieves at that,	
	And, in that kind, swears you do more usurp	
	Than doth your brother that hath banish'd you.	
	To-day my Lord of Amiens, and myself,	
	Did steal behind him as he lay along	30
	Under an oak, whose antique root peeps out	
	Upon the brook that brawls along this wood,	
	To the which place a poor sequester'd stag,	
	That from the hunter's aim had ta'en a hurt,	
	Did come to languish; and indeed, my lord,	
	The wretched animal heav'd forth such groans,	
	That their discharge did stretch his leathern coat	
	Almost to bursting, and the big round tears	
	Cours'd one another down his innocent nose	
	In piteous chase: and thus the hairy fool,	40
	Much marked of the melancholy Jaques,	
	Stood on the extremest verge of the swift brook,	
	Augmenting it with tears.	
Duke Senior	But what said Jaques?	
	Did he not moralise this spectacle?	
First Lord	O, yes, into a thousand similes.	
	First, for his weeping into the needless stream;	
	'Poor deer,' quoth he, 'thou mak'st a testament	
	As wordlings do, giving thy sum of more	
	To that which had too much:' then, being there alone,	[49-52]
	Left and abandon'd of his velvet friend;	50
	''Tis right,' quoth he; 'thus misery doth part	
	The flux of company.' Anon a careless herd,	
	Full of the pasture, jumps along by him	
	And never stays to greet him; 'Ay,' quoth Jaques,	
	'Sweep on, you fat and greasy citizens;	[55-57]
	'Tis just the fashion; wherefore do you look	
	Upon that poor and broken bankrupt there?	
	Thus most invectively he pierceth through	
	The body of the country, city, court,	
	Yea, and of this our life, swearing that we	60

---

24 **forked heads:** arrows
32 **brawl:** make a noise of conflict in its rapid course over stones, etc.
52 **flux:** flood

Are mere usurpers, tyrants, and what's worse,
To fright the animals, and to kill them up
In their assign'd and native dwelling-place.

Duke Senior And did you leave him in this contemplation?

Second Lord We did, my lord, weeping and commenting
Upon the sobbing deer.

Duke Senior   Show me the place!
I love to cope him in these sullen fits,
For then he's full of matter.

First Lord I'll bring you to him straight.   *Exeunt*

Scene 2   [Scene 9]

A room in the palace
Enter Duke Frederick, with Lords

Frederick Can it be possible that no man saw them?
It cannot be; some villains of my court
Are of consent and sufferance in this.

First Lord I cannot hear of any that did see her;
The ladies, her attendants of her chamber,
Saw her a-bed, and in the morning early
They found the bed untreasur'd of their mistress.

Second Lord My Lord, the roynish clown, at whom so oft   [8]
Your Grace was wont to laugh, is also missing;
Hisperia, the princess' gentlewoman,   10
Confesses that she secretly o'erheard
Your daughter and her cousin much commend
The parts and graces of the wrestler
That did but lately foil the sinewy Charles,
And she believes, wherever they are gone,
That youth is surely in their company.

Frederick Send to his brother, fetch that gallant hither,   [17]
If he be absent, bring his brother to me,
I'll make him find him. Do this suddenly;
And let not search and inquisition quail   20
To bring again these foolish runaways.   *Exeunt*

---

67 **cope:** encounter
3 **sufferance:** permission
8 **roynish:** mangy

35

Scene 3 [Scene 10]

Before Oliver's house
Enter Orlando and Adam, meeting

Orlando	Who's there?	
Adam	What, my young master? O my gentle master,	[2-4]
	O my sweet master, O you memory	
	Of old Sir Rowland! Why, what make you here?	
	Why are you virtuous? Why do people love you?	[5-6]
	And wherefore are you gentle, strong, and valiant?	
	Why would you be so fond to overcome	
	The bonny priser of the humorous Duke?	
	Your praise is come too swiftly home before you.	
	Know you not, master, to some kind of men	10
	Their graces serve them but as enemies?	
	No more do yours: your virtues, gentle master,	[12-13]
	Are sanctified and holy traitors to you.	
	O, what a world is this, when what is comely	
	Envenoms him that bears it!	
Orlando	Why, what's the matter?	
Adam	O unhappy youth,	
	Come not within these doors: within this roof	
	The enemy of all your graces lives,	
	Your brother, no, no brother, yet the son,	[19-21]
	Yet not the son, I will not call him son,	20
	Of him I was about to call his father,	
	Hath heard your praises, and this night he means	
	To burn the lodging where you use to lie,	
	And you within it. If he fail of that,	
	He will have other means to cut you off.	
	I overheard him; and his practices.	
	This is no place, this house is but a butchery:	
	Abhor it, fear it, do not enter it.	
Orlando	Why, whither, Adam, wouldst thou have me go?	
Adam	No matter whither, so you come not here.	30
Orlando	What, wouldst thou have me go and beg my food?	
	Or with a base and boisterous sword enforce	
	A thievish living on the common road?	
	This I must do, or know not what to do:	

---

8 **priser:** prizefighter

Yet this I will not do, do how I can;
I rather will subject me to the malice
Of a diverted blood, and bloody brother.

Adam   But do not so. I have five hundred crowns,
The thrifty hire I sav'd under your father,
Which I did store to be my foster-nurse,   40
When service should in my old limbs lie lame,
And unregarded age in corners thrown;
Take that, and He that doth the ravens feed,
Yea, providently caters for the sparrow,
Be comfort to my age! Here is the gold,
All this I give you, let me be your servant;
Though I look old, yet I am strong and lusty;   [47-52]
For in my youth I never did apply
Hot and rebellious liquors in my blood,
Nor did not with unbashful forehead woo   50
The means of weakness and debility;
Therefore my age is as a lusty winter,
Frosty, but kindly. Let me go with you,
I'll do the service of a younger man
In all your business and necessities.

Orlando   O good old man, how well in thee appears
The constant service of the antique world,
When service sweat for duty, not for meed!
Thou art not for the fashion of these times,
Where none will sweat, but for promotion,   60
And having that do choke their service up,
Even with the having; it is not so with thee.
But, poor old man, thou prun'st a rotten tree,
That cannot so much as a blossom yield,
In lieu of all thy pains and husbandry.
But come thy ways, we'll go along together,
And ere we have thy youthful wages spent,
We'll light upon some settled low content.

Adam   Master, go on, and I will follow thee
To the last gasp, with truth and loyalty.   70
From seventeen years, till now almost fourscore
Here lived I, but now live here no more.
At seventeen years, many their fortunes seek,
But at fourscore, it is too late a week:
Yet fortune cannot recompense me better
Than to die well, and not my master's debtor. *Exeunt*

---

39 **hire:** wages
58 **meed:** reward

Scene 4 [Scene 11]

The Forest of Arden
Enter Rosalind for Ganymede, Celia for Aliena, and Touchstone

Rosalind	O Jupiter, how weary are my spirits!
Touchstone	I care not for my spirits, if my legs were not weary.
Rosalind	I could find in my heart to disgrace my man's apparel
	and to cry like a woman, but I must comfort the
	weaker vessel, as doublet and hose ought to show
	itself courageous to petticoat; therefore courage,
	good Aliena.
Celia	I pray you bear with me; I cannot go no further.
Touchstone	For my part, I had rather bear with you than bear
	you: yet I should bear no cross if I did bear you, [10-11]
	for I think you have no money in your purse.
Rosalind	Well, this is the Forest of Arden.
Touchstone	Ay, now am I in Arden, the more fool I; when I
	was at home I was in a better place, but travellers
	must be content.
Rosalind	Ay, be so, good Touchstone.

Enter Corin and Silvius

	Look you, who comes here; a young man and an old	[17-18]
	in solemn talk.	
Corin	That is the way to make her scorn you still.	
Silvius	O Corin, that thou knew'st how I do love her!	20
Corin	I partly guess; for I have lov'd ere now.	
Silvius	No, Corin, being old, thou canst not guess,	
	Though in thy youth thou wast as true a lover	
	As ever sigh'd upon a midnight pillow.	
	But if thy love were ever like to mine, –	
	As sure I think did never man love so, –	
	How many actions most ridiculous	
	Hast thou been drawn to by thy fantasy?	
Corin	Into a thousand that I have forgotten.	
Silvius	O, thou didst then ne'er love so heartily,	30
	If thou remember'st not the slightest folly,	
	That ever love did make thee run into,	
	Thou hast not lov'd.	
	Or if thou hast not sat as I do now,	

Rosalind and Celia with Touchstone, played by Lewis Gordon

	Wearing thy hearer in thy mistress' praise,	[35]
	Thou hast not lov'd.	
	Or if thou hast not broke from company,	
	Abruptly as my passion now makes me,	
	Thou hast not lov'd.	
	O Phebe, Phebe, Phebe! *Exit*	40
Rosalind	Alas, poor shepherd! Searching of thy wound,	
	I have by hard adventure found mine own.	
Touchstone	And I mine. I remember when I was in love, I	
	broke my sword upon a stone, and bid him take that	
	for coming a-night to Jane Smile, and I remember	[45]
	the kissing of her batler, and the cow's dugs that	[46]
	her pretty chopt hands had milked: and I remember	
	the wooing of a peascod instead of her, from whom	
	I took two cods, and, giving her them again, said	[49]
	with weeping tears 'Wear these for my sake.' We	50
	that are true lovers run into strange capers; but as	
	all is mortal in nature, so is all nature in love mortal	
	in folly.	
Rosalind	Thou speak'st wiser than thou art ware of.	
Touchstone	Nay, I shall ne'er be ware of mine own wit, till I	
	break my shins against it.	
Rosalind	Jove, Jove! This shepherd's passion	
	Is much upon my fashion.	
Touchstone	And mine, but it grows something stale with me.	
Celia	I pray you, one of you question yond man,	60
	If he for gold will give us any food;	
	I faint almost to death.	
Touchstone	Holla; you clown!	
Rosalind	Peace, fool, he's not thy kinsman.	
Corin	Who calls?	
Touchstone	Your betters, sir.	
Corin	Else are they very wretched.	
Rosalind	Peace, I say. Good even to you, friend.	
Corin	And to you, gentle sir, and to you all.	
Rosalind	I prithee, shepherd, if that love or gold	
	Can in this desert place buy entertainment,	
	Bring us where we may rest ourselves, and feed:	
	Here's a young maid with travel much oppress'd,	70
	And faints for succour.	

46 **batler:** a wooden club used by washerwomen to beat clothes
47 **chopt:** chapped
48 **peascod:** peapod associated with wooing and considered lucky

Corin	Fair sir, I pity her,	
	And wish, for her sake more than for mine own,	
	My fortunes were more able to relieve her;	
	But I am shepherd to another man,	
	And do not shear the fleeces that I graze:	
	My master is of churlish disposition,	[76-78]
	And little recks to find the way to heaven	
	By doing deeds of hospitality:	
	Besides, his cote, his flocks, and bounds of feed	[79]
	Are now on sale, and at our sheepcote now,	80
	By reason of his absence, there is nothing	
	That you will feed on; but what is, come see,	
	And in my voice most welcome shall you be.	
Rosalind	What is he that shall buy his flock and pasture?	
Corin	That young swain that you saw here but erewhile,	
	That little cares for buying any thing.	
Rosalind	I pray thee, if it stand with honesty,	
	Buy thou the cottage, pasture, and the flock,	
	And thou shalt have to pay for it of us.	
Celia	And we will mend thy wages. I like this place,	90
	And willingly could waste my time in it.	
Corin	Assuredly the thing is to be sold:	
	Go with me, if you like upon report	
	The soil, the profit, and this kind of life,	
	I will your very faithful feeder be,	
	And buy it with your gold right suddenly. *Exeunt*	

Nicholas Pennell as Jaques

Scene 5

Another part of the Forest of Arden
Enter Amiens, Jaques, and others

SONG

Amiens
    Under the greenwood tree,
      Who loves to lie with me,
        And turn his merry note,
          Unto the sweet bird's throat:
    Come hither, come hither, come hither:
      Here shall he see
      No enemy,
    But winter and rough weather.

Jaques More, more, I prithee, more.

Amiens It will make you melancholy, Monsieur Jaques. 10

Jaques I thank it. More, I prithee, more; I can suck
melancholy out of a song, as a weasel sucks eggs.
More, I prithee, more.

Amiens My voice is ragged, I know I cannot please you.

Jaques I do not desire you to please me, I do desire you to sing:
come, more, another stanzo. Call you 'em stanzos?

Amiens What you will, Monsieur Jaques.

Jaques Nay, I care not for their names, they owe me
nothing. Will you sing?

Amiens More at your request than to please myself. 20

Jaques Well then, if ever I thank any man, I'll thank you:
but that they call compliment is like the encounter of
two dog-apes: and when a man thanks me heartily, [23-25]
methinks I have given him a penny, and he renders
me the beggarly thanks. Come, sing; and you that
will not, hold your tongues.

Amiens Well, I'll end the song. Sirs, cover the while,
the Duke will drink under this tree. He hath been
all this day to look you.

Jaques And I have been all this day to avoid him. He is 30
too disputable for my company: I think of as
many matters as he, but I give heaven thanks, and
make no boast of them. Come, warble, come.

---

23 **dog-apes:** dog-faced baboons

Amiens singing "Under the Greenwood Tree"

SONG

	Who doth ambition shun,	*All together here*

Who doth ambition shun,   *All together here*
And loves to live i' the sun:
    Seeking the food he eats,
        And pleased with what he gets:
Come hither, come hither, come hither:
        Here shall he see
        No enemy,   40
    But winter and rough weather.

Jaques   I'll give you a verse to this note, that I made yester-
day in despite of my invention.

Amiens   And I'll sing it.

Jaques   Thus it goes: –

            If it do come to pass,
                That any man turn ass,
            Leaving his wealth and ease,
            A stubborn will to please,
        Ducdame, ducdame, ducdame: [50]
            Here shall he see,
            Gross fools as he,
        And if he will come to me.

Amiens   What's that 'ducdame'?

Jaques   'Tis a Greek invocation, to call fools into a circle.
I'll go sleep, if I can; if I cannot, I'll rail against all
the first-born of Egypt.

Amiens   And I'll go seek the Duke; his banquet is pre-   [58-59]
pared.   *Exeunt severally*

Adam: "Dear Master, I can go no further."

Scene 6

Enter Orlando and Adam

Adam   Dear master, I can go no further: O, I die for
food! Here lie I down, and measure out my grave.
Farewell, kind master.

Orlando   Why, how now, Adam? No greater heart in thee?
Live a little, comfort a little, cheer thyself a little.
If this uncouth forest yield any thing savage, I will
either be food for it, or bring it for food to thee.
Thy conceit is nearer death than thy powers. For my   [8]
sake be comfortable, hold death awhile at the arm's
end: I will here be with thee presently, and if I   10
bring thee not something to eat, I will give thee
leave to die: but if thou diest before I come, thou art
a mocker of my labour. Well said! Thou look'st
cheerly, and I'll be with thee quickly. Yet thou
liest in the bleak air. Come, I will bear thee to some
shelter, and thou shalt not die for lack of a dinner,
if there live any thing in this desert. Cheerly, good
Adam!   *Exeunt*

Scene 7

A table set out. Enter Duke Senior, Amiens, and Lords
like outlaws

Duke Senior	I think he be transform'd into a beast,
	For I can no where find him, like a man.
First Lord	My lord, he is but even now gone hence;
	Here was he merry, hearing of a song.
Duke Senior	If he, compact of jars, grow musical,
	We shall have shortly discord in the spheres. [6]
	Go, seek him, tell him I would speak with him.

Enter Jaques

First Lord	He saves my labour by his own approach.
Duke Senior	Why, how now, monsieur? What a life is this,
	That your poor friends must woo your company? 10
	What, you look merrily!
Jaques	A fool, a fool, I met a fool i' the forest.
	A motley fool – a miserable world! –
	As I do live by food, I met a fool,
	Who laid him down, and bask'd him in the sun,
	And rail'd on Lady Fortune in good terms,
	In good set terms, and yet a motley fool.
	'Good morrow, fool,' quoth I. 'No, sir,' quoth he,
	'Call me not fool, till heaven hath sent me
	fortune:'
	And then he drew a dial from his poke, 20
	And looking on it, with lack-lustre eye,
	Says, very wisely, 'It is ten o'clock:
	Thus we may see,' quoth he, 'how the world wags:
	'Tis but an hour ago since it was nine;
	And after one hour more, 'twill be eleven;
	And so from hour to hour, we ripe, and ripe,
	And then from hour to hour, we rot, and rot,
	And thereby hangs a tale.' When I did hear
	The motley fool thus moral on the time,
	My lungs began to crow like chanticleer, 30
	That fools should be so deep-contemplative;
	And I did laugh, sans intermission

---

5 **compact of jars:** full of discord
20 **poke:** pocket
29 **moral:** philosophize

	An hour by his dial. O noble fool, A worthy fool! Motley's the only wear.	
Duke Senior	What fool is this?	
Jaques	O worthy fool! One that hath been a courtier, And says, if ladies be but young, and fair, They have the gift to know it. And in his brain, Which is as dry as the remainder biscuit After a voyage, he hath strange places cramm'd With observation, the which he vents In mangled forms. O that I were a fool! I am ambitious for a motley coat.	40
Duke Senior	Thou shalt have one.	
Jaques	It is my only suit, Provided that you weed your better judgements Of all opinion that grows rank in them That I am wise. I must have liberty Withal, as large a charter as the wind, To blow on whom I please, for so fools have; And they that are most galled with my folly,	50

They most must laugh. And why, sir, must they so?　　[51-57]
The 'why' is plain, as way to parish church:
He that a fool doth very wisely hit
Doth very foolishly, although he smart,
Not to seem senseless of the bob: if not,
The wise man's folly is anatomized
Even by the squandering glances of the fool.
Invest me in my motley; give me leave
To speak my mind, and I will through and through
Cleanse the foul body of the infected world,　　60
If they will patiently receive my medicine.

Duke Senior	Fie on thee! I can tell what thou wouldst do.	
Jaques	What, for a counter, would I do but good?	
Duke Senior	Most mischievous foul sin, in chiding sin: For thou thyself hast been a libertine, As sensual as the brutish sting itself; And all the embossed sores, and headed evils, That thou with license of free foot hast caught, Wouldst thou disgorge into the general world.	
Jaques	Why, who cries out on pride, That can therein tax any private party? Doth it not flow as hugely as the sea,	70

55　**bob:** bitter jest
63　**counter:** worthless coin

Till that the weary very means do ebb?
What woman in the city do I name,   [74-87]
When that I say the city-woman bears
The cost of princes on unworthy shoulders?
Who can come in, and say that I mean her,
When such a one as she, such is her neighbour?
Or what is he of basest function,
That says his bravery is not on my cost,   80
Thinking that I mean him, but therein suits
His folly to the mettle of my speech?
There then; how then? What then? Let me see wherein
My tongue hath wrong'd him: if it do him right,
Then he hath wrong'd himself; if he be free,
Why then my taxing like a wild-goose flies,
Unclaim'd of any man. But who comes here?

Enter Orlando, with his sword drawn

Orlando	Forbear, and eat no more.
Jaques	Why, I have eat none yet.
Orlando	Nor shalt not, till necessity be serv'd.
Jaques	Of what kind should this cock come of? 90
Duke Senior	Art thou thus bolden'd, man, by thy distress?
	Or else a rude despiser of good manners,
	That in civility thou seem'st so empty?
Orlando	You touch'd my vein at first; the thorny point
	Of bare distress, hath ta'en from me the show
	Of smooth civility: yet am I inland bred,
	And know some nurture. But forbear, I say,
	He dies that touches any of this fruit,
	Till I, and my affairs, are answered.
Jaques	An you will not be answer'd with reason, I must die. 100
Duke Senior	What would you have? Your gentleness shall force,
	More than your force move us to gentleness.
Orlando	I almost die for food, and let me have it.
Duke Senior	Sit down and feed, and welcome to our table.
Orlando	Speak you so gently? Pardon me I pray you,
	I thought that all things had been savage here,
	And therefore put I on the countenance
	Of stern commandment. But whate'er you are
	That in this desert inaccessible,
	Under the shade of melancholy boughs, 110

---

79 **function:** occupation
82 **mettle:** spirit

Orlando interrupts Jaques, Duke Senior, played by William Needles, Amiens, and the Forest Lords: "Forbear, and eat no more."

	Lose and neglect the creeping hours of time;	
	If ever you have look'd on better days;	
	If ever been where bells have knoll'd to church;	
	If ever sat at any good man's feast;	
	If ever from your eyelids wip'd a tear,	
	And know what 'tis to pity, and be pitied;	
	Let gentleness my strong enforcement be:	
	In the which hope I blush, and hide my sword.	
Duke Senior	True is it, that we have seen better days,	
	And have with holy bell been knoll'd to church,	120
	And sat at good men's feasts, and wip'd our eyes	
	Of drops, that sacred pity hath engender'd:	
	And therefore sit you down in gentleness,	
	And take upon command what help we have	
	That to your wanting may be minister'd.	
Orlando	Then but forbear your food a little while,	
	Whiles, like a doe, I go to find my fawn,	[127-28]
	And give it food. There is an old poor man,	
	Who after me hath many a weary step	
	Limp'd in pure love: till he be first suffic'd,	130
	Oppress'd with two weak evils, age, and hunger,	
	I will not touch a bit.	
Duke Senior	Go find him out:	
	And we will nothing waste till you return.	
Orlando	I thank ye, and be blest for your good comfort!	

Exit

Duke Senior	Thou seest, we are not all alone unhappy.	
	This wide and universal theatre	
	Presents more woeful pageants than the scene	
	Wherein we play in.	
Jaques	All the world's a stage,	
	And all the men and women, merely players;	
	They have their exits and their entrances,	140
	And one man in his time plays many parts,	
	His acts being seven ages. At first the infant,	
	Mewling, and puking in the nurse's arms:	
	Then the whining school-boy with his satchel	
	And shining morning face, creeping like snail	
	Unwillingly to school. And then the lover,	
	Sighing like furnace, with a woeful ballad	

◄ Jaques: "All the world's a stage."

Made to his mistress' eyebrow. Then, a soldier,
Full of strange oaths, and bearded like the pard,
Jealous in honour, sudden, and quick in quarrel,   150
Seeking the bubble reputation
Even in the cannon's mouth: and then, the justice,
In fair round belly, with good capon lin'd,
With eyes severe, and beard of formal cut,
Full of wise saws, and modern instances,
And so he plays his part. The sixth age shifts
Into the lean and slipper'd pantaloon,
With spectacles on nose, and pouch on side,
His youthful hose well sav'd, a world too wide,
For his shrunk shank, and his big manly voice,   160
Turning again toward childish treble, pipes,
And whistles in his sound. Last scene of all,
That ends this strange eventful history,
Is second childishness, and mere oblivion,
Sans teeth, sans eyes, sans taste, sans every thing.

Re-enter Orlando, with Adam

Duke Senior   Welcome; set down your venerable burthen,
And let him feed.
Orlando   I thank you most for him.
Adam   So had you need,
I scarce can speak to thank you for myself.
Duke Senior   Welcome, fall to: I will not trouble you   170
As yet to question you about your fortunes.
Give us some music, and, good cousin, sing.
Amiens   (*sings*) Blow, blow, thou winter wind,
Thou art not so unkind,
    As man's ingratitude;
Thy tooth is not so keen,
Because thou art not seen,
    Although thy breath be rude.
    Heigh-ho! Sing, heigh-ho! Unto the green holly:
    Most friendship is feigning, most loving, mere folly: 180
Then, heigh-ho, the holly!
    This life is most jolly.

>Freeze, freeze, thou bitter sky,
>That dost not bite so nigh
>　As benefits forgot:
>Though thou the waters warp,
>Thy sting is not so sharp,
>　As friend remember'd not.
>　Heigh-ho! sing, &c.

Duke Senior　If that you were the good Sir Rowland's son, 190
As you have whisper'd faithfully you were,
And as mine eye doth his effigies witness, [192-93]
Most truly limn'd, and living in your face,
Be truly welcome hither. I am the Duke
That lov'd your father; the residue of your fortune,
Go to my cave, and tell me. Good old man,
Thou art right welcome, as thy master is.
Support him by the arm. Give me your hand,
And let me all your fortunes understand.　*Exeunt*

Act Third

Scene 1

[Scene 15]

A room in the palace
Enter Duke Frederick, Lords, and Oliver

Frederick	Not see him since? Sir, sir, that cannot be:
	But were I not the better part made mercy,
	I should not seek an absent argument
	Of my revenge, thou present. But look to it,
	Find out thy brother wheresoe'er he is,
	Seek him with candle; bring him dead, or living,
	Within this twelvemonth, or turn thou no more
	To seek a living in our territory.
	Thy lands and all things that thou dost call thine,
	Worth seizure, do we seize into our hands,
	Till thou canst quit thee by thy brother's mouth,
	Of what we think against thee.
Oliver	O that your Highness knew my heart in this!
	I never lov'd my brother in my life.
Frederick	More villain thou. Well, push him out of doors,
	And let my officers of such a nature
	Make an extent upon his house and lands.
	Do this expediently, and turn him going. *Exeunt*

10

Scene 2

The forest
Enter Orlando, with a paper

Orlando   Hang there, my verse, in witness of my love,
  And thou, thrice-crowned queen of night, survey [2]
With thy chaste eye, from thy pale sphere above,
  Thy huntress' name that my full life doth sway.
O Rosalind! These trees shall be my books,
  And in their barks my thoughts I'll character,
That every eye, which in this forest looks,
  Shall see thy virtue witness'd every where.
Run, run, Orlando, carve on every tree,
The fair, the chaste, and unexpressive she. *Exit* 10

INTERVAL

Enter Corin and Touchstone

Corin And how like you this shepherd's life, Master
  Touchstone?
Touchstone Truly, shepherd, in respect of itself, it is a good
  life; but in respect that it is a shepherd's life, it is
  naught. In respect that it is solitary, I like it very [15]
  well; but in respect that it is private, it is a very [16]
  vile life. Now, in respect it is in the fields, it pleaseth
  me well; but in respect it is not in the court, it is
  tedious. As it is a spare life, look you, it fits my
  humour well; but as there is no more plenty in it, 20
  it goes much against my stomach. Hast any philo-
  sophy in thee, shepherd?
Corin No more but that I know the more one sickens the
  worse at ease he is; and that he that wants money, [24-25]
  means, and content, is without three good friends;
  that the property of rain is to wet, and fire to burn:
  that good pasture makes fat sheep: and that a great

	cause of the night is lack of the sun; that he that	[28-30]
	hath learned no wit by nature, nor art, may complain	
	of good breeding, or comes of a very dull kindred.	30
Touchstone	Such a one is a natural philosopher. Wast ever in	
	court, shepherd?	
Corin	No, truly.	
Touchstone	Then thou art damn'd.	
Corin	Nay, I hope.	
Touchstone	Truly, thou art damn'd, like an ill-roasted egg, all	[36-37]
	on one side.	
Corin	For not being at court? Your reason.	
Touchstone	Why, if thou never wast at court, thou never	
	saw'st good manners: if thou never saw'st good	40
	manners, then thy manners must be wicked, and	
	wickedness is sin, and sin is damnation. Thou art	
	in a parlous state, shepherd.	
Corin	Not a whit, Touchstone; those that are good	
	manners at the court are as ridiculous in the country	
	as the behaviour of the country is most mockable at	
	the court. You told me, you salute not at the court,	
	but you kiss your hands; that courtesy would be	
	uncleanly if courtiers were shepherds.	
Touchstone	Instance, briefly; come, instance.	50
Corin	Why, we are still handling our ewes, and their fells	[51]
	you know are greasy.	
Touchstone	Why, do not your courtier's hands sweat? And	
	is not the grease of a mutton as wholesome as	
	the sweat of a man? Shallow, shallow: a better	
	instance, I say; come.	
Corin	Besides, our hands are hard.	
Touchstone	Your lips will feel them the sooner. Shallow again:	
	a more sounder instance, come.	
Corin	And they are often tarr'd over, with the surgery of	60
	our sheep; and would you have us kiss tar? The	
	courtier's hands are perfum'd with civet.	
Touchstone	Most shallow man! Thou worm's-meat in respect of	[63-64]
	a good piece of flesh indeed! Learn of the wise and	
	perpend: civet is of a baser birth than tar, the very	
	uncleanly flux of a cat. Mend the instance, shepherd.	
Corin	You have too courtly a wit, for me; I'll rest.	
Touchstone	Wilt thou rest damn'd? God help thee, shallow	
	man! God make incision in thee! Thou art raw.	[69]

---

43 **parlous:** dangerous
65 **perpend:** consider
66 **flux:** discharge

Corin	Sir, I am a true labourer, I earn that I eat; get that	70
	I wear; owe no man hate, envy no man's happiness:	
	glad of other men's good, content with my harm:	
	and the greatest of my pride is to see my ewes graze,	
	and my lambs suck.	
Touchstone	That is another simple sin in you, to bring the ewes	
	and the rams together, and to offer to get your	
	living by the copulation of cattle, to be bawd to a	
	bell-wether, and to betray a she-lamb of a twelve-	
	month to a crooked-pated old cuckoldly ram, out of	
	all reasonable match. If thou beest not damn'd for	80
	this, the devil himself will have no shepherds; I	
	cannot see else how thou shouldst 'scape.	
Corin	Here comes young Master Ganymede, my new	
	mistress's brother.	

Enter Rosalind, with a paper, reading   [Scene 18]

Rosalind	From the east to western Ind,	
	No jewel is like Rosalind.	
	Her worth, being mounted on the wind,	
	Through all the world bears Rosalind.	
	All the pictures fairest lin'd	
	Are but black to Rosalind.	90
	Let no face be kept in mind,	
	But the fair of Rosalind.	
Touchstone	I'll rhyme you so, eight years together; dinners,	
	and suppers, and sleeping-hours excepted: it is the	[94-95]
	right butter-women's rank to market.	
Rosalind	Out, fool!	
Touchstone	For a taste:	
	If a hart do lack a hind,	
	Let him seek out Rosalind.	
	If the cat will after kind,	100
	So be sure will Rosalind,	
	Winter garments must be lin'd,	
	So must slender Rosalind.	
	They that reap must sheaf and bind,	[104-05]
	Then to cart with Rosalind.	
	Sweetest nut hath sourest rind,	
	Such a nut is Rosalind.	
	He that sweetest rose will find,	
	Must find love's prick, and Rosalind.	

---

98   **hart:** male deer

TOUGHSTONE 'iN ARDEN '

	This is the very false gallop of verses; why do you infect yourself with them?	110
Rosalind	Peace, you dull fool! I found them on a tree.	
Touchstone	Truly the tree yields bad fruit.	
Rosalind	I'll graff it with you, and then I shall graff it with a medlar: then it will be the earliest fruit i' the country; for you'll be rotten ere you be half ripe, and that's the right virtue of the medlar.	[114-15]
Touchstone	You have said; but whether wisely or no, let the forest judge.	

Enter Celia, with a writing

Rosalind	Peace!	120
	Here comes my sister reading. Stand aside.	
Celia	(reads) Why should this desert be,	

        For it is unpeopled? No;
Tongues I'll hang on every tree,
        That shall civil sayings show:
Some, how brief the life of man   [126-31]
        Runs his erring pilgrimage,
That the stretching of a span
        Buckles in his sum of age;
Some, of violated vows,   130
        'Twixt the souls of friend and friend:
But upon the fairest boughs,
        Or at every sentence end,
Will I Rosalinda write,
        Teaching all that read, to know
The quintessence of every sprite,
        Heaven would in little show.
Therefore Heaven Nature charg'd
        That one body should be fill'd
With all graces wide-enlarg'd: 140
        Nature presently distill'd
Helen's cheek, but not her heart,   [142-45]
        Cleopatra's majesty,
Atalanta's better part,
        Sad Lucretia's modesty.

---

114 **graff:** graft
115 **medlar:** a tree whose apple-like fruit is eaten only when decayed
141 **presently:** immediately

Rosalind with Orlando's verses: "I found them on a tree."

	Thus Rosalind of many parts	[146-49]
	By heavenly synod was devis'd;	
	Of many faces, eyes, and hearts,	
	To have the touches dearest priz'd.	
	Heaven would that she these gifts should have,	150
	And I to live and die her slave.	
Rosalind	O most gentle Jupiter, what tedious homily of love	
	have you wearied your parishioners withal, and never	
	cried 'Have patience, good people'!	
Celia	How now? Back, friends. Shepherd, go off a little.	
	Go with him, sirrah.	
Touchstone	Come, shepherd, let us make an honourable retreat,	
	though not with bag and baggage, yet with scrip and	
	scrippage.	

Exeunt Corin and Touchstone

Celia	Didst thou hear these verses?	160
Rosalind	O, yes, I heard them all, and more too, for some of	
	them had in them more feet than the verses would bear.	
Celia	That's no matter: the feet might bear the verses.	
Rosalind	Ay, but the feet were lame, and could not bear them-	
	selves without the verse, and therefore stood lamely	
	in the verse.	
Celia	But didst thou hear without wondering how thy	
	name should be hang'd and carved upon these trees?	
Rosalind	I was seven of the nine days out of the wonder,	170
	before you came: for look here what I found on a	
	palm tree; I was never so be-rhym'd since Pytha-	[172-73]
	goras' time, that I was an Irish rat, which I can hardly	
	remember.	
Celia	Trow you who hath done this?	
Rosalind	Is it a man?	
Celia	And a chain that you once wore about his neck.	
	Change you colour?	
Rosalind	I prithee, who?	
Celia	O Lord, Lord, it is a hard matter for friends to meet;	[180-81]
	but mountains may be remov'd with earthquakes,	
	and so encounter.	
Rosalind	Nay, but who is it?	
Celia	Is it possible?	
Rosalind	Nay, I prithee now, with most petitionary vehe-	
	mence, tell me who it is.	

---

147 **synod:** ecclesiastical assembly; in astronomical sense, conjunction

CELIA IN ARDEN

Celia	O wonderful, wonderful, and most wonderful wonderful, and yet again wonderful, and after that out of all whooping!
Rosalind	Good my complexion, dost thou think, though I am caparisoned like a man, I have a doublet and hose in my disposition? One inch of delay more is a South-sea of discovery. I prithee, tell me who is it quickly, and speak apace: I would thou couldst stammer, that thou might'st pour this conceal'd man out of thy mouth, as wine comes out of a narrow-mouth'd bottle; either too much at once, or none at all. I prithee, take the cork out of thy mouth, that I may drink thy tidings.
Celia	So you may put a man in your belly.
Rosalind	Is he of God's making? What manner of man? Is his head worth a hat? Or his chin worth a beard?
Celia	Nay, he hath but a little beard.
Rosalind	Why, God will send more, if the man will be thankful; let me stay the growth of his beard, if thou delay me not the knowledge of his chin.
Celia	It is young Orlando, that tripped up the wrestler's heels, and your heart, both in an instant.
Rosalind	Nay, but the devil take mocking: speak sad brow, and true maid.
Celia	I' faith, coz, 'tis he.
Rosalind	Orlando?
Celia	Orlando.
Rosalind	Alas the day, what shall I do with my doublet and hose? What did he when thou saw'st him? What said he? How looked he? Wherein went he? What makes he here? Did he ask for me? Where remains he? How parted he with thee? And when shalt thou see him again? Answer me in one word.
Celia	You must borrow me Gargantua's mouth first: 'tis a word too great for any mouth of this age's size; to say ay and no, to these particulars, is more than to answer in a catechism.

190

200

210

220

[222-24]

---

221 **Gargantua:** Rabelais's giant

Rosalind	But doth he know that I am in this forest, and in man's apparel? Looks he as freshly as he did the day he wrestled?
Celia	It is as easy to count atomies as to resolve the pro-positions of a lover: but take a taste of my finding him, and relish it with good observance. I found him under a tree like a dropped acorn.
Rosalind	It may well be called Jove's tree, when it drops forth such fruit.
Celia	Give me audience, good madam.
Rosalind	Proceed.
Celia	There lay he stretched along like a wounded knight.
Rosalind	Though it be pity to see such a sight, it well becomes the ground.
Celia	Cry 'holla' to thy tongue, I prithee; it curvets unseasonably. He was furnish'd like a hunter.
Rosalind	O ominous, he comes to kill my heart.
Celia	I would sing my song without a burden: thou bring'st me out of tune.
Rosalind	Do you not know I am a woman? When I think, I must speak. Sweet, say on.
Celia	You bring me out. Soft, comes he not here?

Enter Orlando and Jaques

Rosalind	'Tis he; slink by, and note him.
Jaques	I thank you for your company, but, good faith, I had as lief have been myself alone.
Orlando	And so had I; but yet, for fashion sake, I thank you too, for your society.
Jaques	God buy you, let's meet as little as we can.
Orlando	I do desire we may be better strangers.
Jaques	I pray you, mar no more trees with writing love-songs in their barks.
Orlando	I pray you, mar no moe of my verses with reading them ill-favouredly.
Jaques	Rosalind is your love's name?
Orlando	Yes, just.
Jaques	I do not like her name.
Orlando	There was no thought of pleasing you when she was christen'd.
Jaques	What stature is she of?

230

239 **curvets:** leaps and frisks

Orlando	Just as high as my heart.
Jaques	You are full of pretty answers: have you not been [265-68] acquainted with goldsmiths' wives, and conned them out of rings?
Orlando	Not so; but I answer you right painted cloth, from whence you have studied your questions.
Jaques	You have a nimble wit; I think 'twas made of 270 Atalanta's heels. Will you sit down with me, and we two will rail against our mistress the world, and all our misery.
Orlando	I will chide no breather in the world but myself, against whom I know most faults.
Jaques	The worst fault you have is to be in love.
Orlando	'Tis a fault I will not change, for your best virtue. I am weary of you.
Jaques	By my troth, I was seeking for a fool, when I found you. 280
Orlando	He is drown'd in the brook, look but in, and you shall see him.
Jaques	There I shall see mine own figure.
Orlando	Which I take to be either a fool, or a cipher.
Jaques	I'll tarry no longer with you, farewell, good Signior Love.
Orlando	I am glad of your departure. Adieu, good Monsieur Melancholy.

Exit Jaques

Rosalind	*(aside to Celia)* I will speak to him like a saucy lackey, and under that habit play the knave with 290 him. Do you hear, forester?
Orlando	Very well; what would you?
Rosalind	I pray you, what is 't o'clock?
Orlando	You should ask me what time o' day: there's no clock in the forest.
Rosalind	Then there is no true lover in the forest, else sighing every minute and groaning every hour would detect the lazy foot of Time as well as a clock.
Orlando	And why not the swift foot of Time? Had not that 300 been as proper?
Rosalind	By no means, sir: Time travels in divers paces, with divers persons. I'll tell you who Time ambles

	withal, who Time trots withal, who Time gallops	
	withal, and who he stands still withal.	
Orlando	I prithee, who doth he trot withal?	
Rosalind	Marry, he trots hard with a young maid, between	
	the contract of her marriage, and the day it is	
	solemniz'd; if the interim be but a se'nnight, Time's	[309]
	pace is so hard, that it seems the length of seven	310
	year.	
Orlando	Who ambles Time withal?	
Rosalind	With a priest that lacks Latin, and a rich man that	
	hath not the gout; for the one sleeps easily because	
	he cannot study, and the other lives merrily, because	
	he feels no pain: the one lacking the burden of	[316-18]
	lean and wasteful learning; the other knowing	
	no burden of heavy tedious penury. These Time	
	ambles withal.	
Orlando	Who doth he gallop withal?	320
Rosalind	With a thief to the gallows: for though he go as	
	softly as foot can fall, he thinks himself too soon	
	there.	
Orlando	Who stays it still withal?	
Rosalind	With lawyers in the vacation: for they sleep	
	between term and term, and then they perceive	
	not how Time moves.	
Orlando	Where dwell you, pretty youth?	
Rosalind	With this shepherdess, my sister; here in the skirts	
	of the forest, like fringe upon a petticoat.	330
Orlando	Are you native of this place?	
Rosalind	As the cony that you see dwell where she is kindled.	[332]
Orlando	Your accent is something finer than you could pur-	
	chase in so remov'd a dwelling.	
Rosalind	I have been told so of many: but indeed, an old	
	religious uncle of mine taught me to speak, who	
	was in his youth an inland man, one that knew	
	courtship too well: for there he fell in love. I	
	have heard him read many lectures against it, and	
	I thank God, I am not a woman, to be touch'd	340
	with so many giddy offences as he hath generally	
	tax'd their whole sex withal.	[342]
Orlando	Can you remember any of the principal evils, that	
	he laid to the charge of women?	

Orlando, Celia, and Rosalind: "I am he that is so love-shaked."

Rosalind	There were none principal, they were all like one another, as half-pence are, every one fault seeming monstrous, till his fellow-fault came to match it.
Orlando	I prithee, recount some of them.
Rosalind	No: I will not cast away my physic, but on those that are sick. There is a man haunts the forest, 350 that abuses our young plants with carving Rosalind on their barks; hangs odes upon hawthorns, and elegies on brambles; all, forsooth, deifying the name of Rosalind. If I could meet that fancy-monger, I would give him some good counsel, for he seems to have the quotidian of love upon him.
Orlando	I am he that is so love-shak'd, I pray you tell me your remedy.
Rosalind	There is none of my uncle's marks upon you: he taught me how to know a man in love: in which 360 cage of rushes I am sure you are not prisoner.
Orlando	What were his marks?
Rosalind	A lean cheek, which you have not; a blue eye and sunken, which you have not; an unquestionable spirit, which you have not: a beard neglected, which you have not: (but I pardon you for that, for simply your having in beard is a younger brother's revenue): then your hose should be ungarter'd, your bonnet unbanded, your sleeve unbutton'd, your shoe untied, and every thing about you demonstrat- 370 ing a careless desolation: but you are no such man; you are rather point-device in your accoutrements, as loving yourself, than seeming the lover of any other.
Orlando	Fair youth, I would I could make thee believe I love.
Rosalind	Me believe it? You may as soon make her that you love believe it, which I warrant she is apter to do than to confess she does: That is one of the points, in the which women still give the lie to their consciences. But in good sooth, are you he that 380 hangs the verses on the trees, wherein Rosalind is so admir'd?
Orlando	I swear to thee, youth, by the white hand of Rosalind, I am that he, that unfortunate he.
Rosalind	But are you so much in love as your rhymes speak?

---

356 **quotidian:** daily fever

Orlando	Neither rhyme nor reason can express how much.
Rosalind	Love is merely a madness, and, I tell you, deserves
	as well a dark house, and a whip, as madmen do: [388]
	and the reason why they are not so punish'd and
	cur'd is, that the lunacy is so ordinary, that the 390
	whippers are in love too: yet I profess curing it by
	counsel.
Orlando	Did you ever cure any so?
Rosalind	Yes, one, and in this manner. He was to imagine
	me his love, his mistress; and I set him every day
	to woo me: at which time would I, being but a
	moonish youth, grieve, be effeminate, changeable,
	longing, and liking, proud, fantastical, apish, shallow,
	inconstant, full of tears, full of smiles; for every
	passion something, and for no passion truly any 400
	thing; as boys and women are for the most part
	cattle of this colour: would now like him, now
	loath him; then entertain him, then forswear him;
	now weep for him, then spit at him; that I drave
	my suitor from his mad humour of love, to a living
	humour of madness, which was to forswear the
	full stream of the world, and to live in a nook
	merely monastic. And thus I cur'd him, and this
	way will I take upon me to wash your liver as
	clean as a sound sheep's heart, that there shall not 410
	be one spot of love in 't.
Orlando	I would not be cur'd, youth.
Rosalind	I would cure you, if you would but call me Rosalind
	and come every day to my cote, and woo me.
Orlando	Now, by the faith of my love, I will; tell me where it is.
Rosalind	Go with me to it, and I'll show it you: and by the
	way you shall tell me where in the forest you live.
	Will you go?
Orlando	With all my heart, good youth.
Rosalind	Nay, you must call me Rosalind. Come, sister, 420
	will you go? *Exeunt* [421]

Scene 3 [Scene 20]

The forest
Enter Touchstone and Audrey; Jaques behind

Touchstone	Come apace, good Audrey, I will fetch up your goats, Audrey. And how, Audrey? Am I the man yet? Doth my simple feature content you?.
Audrey	Your features, Lord warrant us: what features?
Touchstone	I am here with thee, and thy goats, as the most capricious poet honest Ovid was among the Goths.
Jaques	*(aside)* O knowledge ill-inhabited, worse than Jove in a thatch'd house!
Touchstone	When a man's verses cannot be understood, nor a man's good wit seconded with the forward child, understanding, it strikes a man more dead than a great reckoning in a little room. Truly, I would the gods had made thee poetical.
Audrey	I do not know what 'poetical' is: is it honest in deed and word? Is it a true thing?
Touchstone	No, truly; for the truest poetry is the most feigning, and lovers are given to poetry: and what they swear in poetry, may be said as lovers, they do feign.
Audrey	Do you wish then that the gods had made me poetical?
Touchstone	I do, truly; for thou swear'st to me thou art honest: now, if thou wert a poet, I might have some hope thou didst feign.
Audrey	Would you not have me honest?
Touchstone	No, truly, unless thou wert hard-favour'd; for honesty coupled to beauty is to have honey a sauce to sugar.
Jaques	*(aside)* A material fool!
Audrey	Well, I am not fair, and therefore I pray the gods make me honest.
Touchstone	Truly, and to cast away honesty upon a foul slut were to put good meat into an unclean dish.

[10-13]

20

30

Audrey, played by Elizabeth Leigh-Milne, and Touchstone

Audrey	I am not a slut, though I thank the gods I am foul.
Touchstone	Well, prais'd be the gods for thy foulness;
	sluttishness may come hereafter. But be it as it may
	be, I will marry thee: and to that end, I have been
	with Sir Oliver Martext, the vicar of the next village,
	who hath promis'd to meet me in this place of the 40
	forest, and to couple us.
Jaques	*(aside)* I would fain see this meeting.
Audrey	Well, the gods give us joy!
Touchstone	Amen. A man may, if he were of a fearful
	heart, stagger in this attempt; for here we have
	no temple but the wood, no assembly but horn-
	beasts. But what though? Courage! As horns [47-59]
	are odious, they are necessary. It is said, 'many a
	man knows no end of his goods:' right: many a
	man has good horns, and knows no end of them. 50
	Well, that is the dowry of his wife, 'tis none of
	his own getting. Horns? – even so: – poor men
	alone? No, no, the noblest deer hath them as
	huge as the rascal: is the single man therefore
	blessed? No, as a wall'd town is more worthier
	than a village, so is the forehead of a married man
	more honourable than the bare brow of a bachelor:
	and by how much defence is better than no skill,
	by so much is a horn more precious than to want.
	Here comes Sir Oliver. [60]

Enter Sir Oliver Martext

	Sir Oliver Martext, you are well met. Will you [61]
	dispatch us here under this tree, or shall we go with
	you to your chapel?
Martext	Is there none here to give the woman?
Touchstone	I will not take her on gift of any man.
Martext	Truly, she must be given, or the marriage is not
	lawful.
Jaques	Proceed, proceed: I'll give her.
Touchstone	Good even, good Master What-ye-call 't: how do
	you, sir? You are very well met: God 'ild you for [70]
	your last company, I am very glad to see you, even
	a toy in hand here, sir: nay, pray be cover'd.

---

72   **toy:** matter of little importance

Jaques	Will you be married, motley?
Touchstone	As the ox hath his bow, sir, the horse his curb,
	and the falcon her bells, so man hath his desires, and
	as pigeons bill, so wedlock would be nibbling.
Jaques	And will you, being a man of your breeding, be
	married under a bush like a beggar? Get you to
	church, and have a good priest that can tell you what
	marriage is; this fellow will but join you together,
	as they join wainscot; then one of you will prove
	a shrunk panel, and like green timber, warp, warp.
Touchstone	*(aside)* I am not in the mind but I were better to
	be married of him than of another, for he is not
	like to marry me well; and not being well married,
	it will be a good excuse for me hereafter, to leave my
	wife.
Jaques	Go thou with me, and let me counsel thee.
Touchstone	Come, sweet Audrey,
	We must be married, or we must live in bawdry.
	Farewell, good Master Oliver: not, –
	O sweet Oliver,
	O brave Oliver,
	Leave me not behind thee:
	but, –
	Wind away,
	Begone, I say,
	I will not to wedding with thee.
	Exeunt Jaques, Touchstone, and Audrey
Martext	'Tis no matter: ne'er a fantastical knave of them
	all shall flout me out of my calling. *Exit*

Line markers in right margin:
[79]
[80]

[88]

[90]

100

Scene 4 [Scene 21]

The forest
Enter Rosalind and Celia

Rosalind	Never talk to me, I will weep.
Celia	Do, I prithee, but yet have the grace to consider
	that tears do not become a man.
Rosalind	But have I not cause to weep?
Celia	As good cause as one would desire, therefore weep.
Rosalind	His very hair is of the dissembling colour.
Celia	Something browner than Judas's: marry, his kisses
	are Judas's own children.
Rosalind	I' faith, his hair is of a good colour.
Celia	An excellent colour: your chestnut was ever the only 10
	colour.
Rosalind	And his kissing is as full of sanctity as the touch of
	holy bread.
Celia	He hath bought a pair of cast lips of Diana. A nun [14]
	of winter's sisterhood kisses not more religiously;
	the very ice of chastity is in them.
Rosalind	But why did he swear he would come this morning,
	and comes not?
Celia	Nay, certainly, there is no truth in him.
Rosalind	Do you think so? 20
Celia	Yes, I think he is not a pick-purse, nor a horse-stealer,
	but for his verity in love, I do think him as concave
	as a covered goblet, or a worm-eaten nut.
Rosalind	Not true in love?
Celia	Yes, when he is in, but I think he is not in.
Rosalind	You have heard him swear downright he was.
Celia	'Was' is not 'is'. Besides, the oath of a lover is
	no stronger than the word of a tapster, they are both
	the confirmer of false reckonings; he attends here
	in the forest on the Duke your father. 30
Rosalind	I met the Duke yesterday, and had much question
	with him: he ask'd me of what parentage I was;
	I told him, of as good as he, so he laugh'd and let
	me go. But what talk we of fathers, when there is
	such a man as Orlando?

28   **tapster:** drawer of ale

Celia and Rosalind: "Never talk to me, I will weep."

Celia	O, that's a brave man, he writes brave verses, speaks
	brave words, swears brave oaths, and breaks them
	bravely, quite traverse athwart the heart of his lover, [38-41]
	as a puisny tilter, that spurs his horse but on one side,
	breaks his staff like a noble goose: but all's brave that 40
	youth mounts, and folly guides. Who comes here?

Enter Corin

Corin	Mistress and master, you have oft inquir'd
	After the shepherd that complain'd of love,
	Who you saw sitting by me on the turf,
	Praising the proud disdainful shepherdess
	That was his mistress.
Celia	Well; and what of him?
Corin	If you will see a pageant truly play'd
	Between the pale complexion of true love
	And the red glow of scorn and proud disdain,
	Go hence a little, and I shall conduct you 50
	If you will mark it.
Rosalind	O, come, let us remove,
	The sight of lovers feedeth those in love:
	Bring us to this sight, and you shall say
	I'll prove a busy actor in their play. *Exeunt*

Scene 5

[Scene 22]

Another part of the forest
Enter Silvius and Phebe

Silvius	Sweet Phebe, do not scorn me, do not, Phebe;
	Say that you love me not, but say not so
	In bitterness; the common executioner,
	Whose heart the accustom'd sight of death makes hard,
	Falls not the axe upon the humbled neck
	But first begs pardon: will you sterner be
	Than he that dies and lives by bloody drops?

---

39 **puisny:** inferior, junior

Enter Rosalind, Celia, and Corin, behind

Phebe	I would not be thy executioner,
	I fly thee, for I would not injure thee:
	Thou tell'st me there is murder in mine eye; 10
	'Tis pretty, sure, and very probable, [11]
	That eyes, that are the frail'st, and softest things,
	Who shut their coward gates on atomies,
	Should be call'd tyrants, butchers, murderers!
	Now I do frown on thee with all my heart,
	And if mine eyes can wound, now let them kill thee:
	Now counterfeit to swoon, why now fall down,
	Or if thou canst not, O, for shame, for shame,
	Lie not, to say mine eyes are murderers!
	Now show the wound mine eye hath made in thee, 20
	Scratch thee but with a pin, and there remains
	Some scar of it; lean upon a rush, [22-24]
	The cicatrice and capable impressure
	Thy palm some moment keeps; but now mine eyes,
	Which I have darted at thee, hurt thee not,
	Nor, I am sure, there is no force in eyes
	That can do hurt.
Silvius	O dear Phebe,
	If ever, – as that ever may be near, –
	You meet in some fresh cheek the power of fancy,
	Then shall you know the wounds invisible 30
	That Love's keen arrows make.
Phebe	But till that time
	Come not thou near me: and when that time comes,
	Afflict me with thy mocks, pity me not,
	As till that time I shall not pity thee.
Rosalind	And why, I pray you? Who might be your mother,
	That you insult, exult, and all at once,
	Over the wretched? What though you have no beauty,
	As, by my faith, I see no more in you
	Than without candle may go dark to bed:
	Must you be therefore proud and pitiless? 40
	Why, what means this? Why do you look on me?
	I see no more in you than in the ordinary
	Of nature's sale-work. 'Od's my little life,

---

23 **cicatrice:** scar of a healed wound

I think she means to tangle my eyes too:
No, faith, proud mistress, hope not after it,
'Tis not your inky brows, your black silk hair,
Your bugle eyeballs, nor your cheek of cream,
That can entame my spirits to your worship:
You foolish shepherd, wherefore do you follow her
Like foggy south, puffing with wind and rain?   50
You are a thousand times a properer man
Than she a woman. 'Tis such fools as you
That makes the world full of ill-favour'd children:
'Tis not her glass, but you, that flatters her,
And out of you she sees herself more proper
Than any of her lineaments can show her:
But, mistress, know yourself, down on your knees,
And thank heaven, fasting, for a good man's love;
For I must tell you friendly in your ear,
Sell when you can, you are not for all markets.   60
Cry the man mercy, love him, take his offer,
Foul is most foul, being foul to be a scoffer.
So take her to thee, shepherd. Fare you well.

Phebe   Sweet youth, I pray you, chide a year together,
I had rather hear you chide than this man woo.

Rosalind   He's fall'n in love with your foulness, and she'll fall
in love with my anger. If it be so, as fast as she
answers thee with frowning looks, I'll sauce her with
bitter words. Why look you so upon me?

Phebe   For no ill will I bear you.   70

Rosalind   I pray you do not fall in love with me,
For I am falser than vows made in wine:
Besides, I like you not: if you will know my house,
'Tis at the tuft of olives, here hard by.
Will you go, sister? Shepherd, ply her hard.
Come, sister. Shepherdess, look on him better,
And be not proud, though all the world could see,
None could be so abus'd in sight as he.
Come, to our flock.

Exeunt Rosalind, Celia and Corin

[Scene 23]

Phebe   Dead shepherd, now I find thy saw of might,   [80-81]
'Who ever lov'd, that lov'd not at first sight?'

Silvius   Sweet Phebe, –

Phebe	Ha; what say'st thou, Silvius?
Silvius	Sweet Phebe, pity me.
Phebe	Why, I am sorry for thee, gentle Silvius.
Silvius	Wherever sorrow is, relief would be:

If you do sorrow at my grief in love,
By giving love, your sorrow, and my grief,
Were both extermin'd.

Phebe   Thou hast my love, is not that neighbourly?

Silvius   I would have you.

Phebe   Why, that were covetousness.   90
Silvius, the time was that I hated thee;
And yet it is not that I bear thee love,
But since that thou canst talk of love so well,
Thy company, which erst was irksome to me,
I will endure; and I'll employ thee too:
But do not look for further recompense
Than thine own gladness, that thou art employ'd.

Silvius   So holy, and so perfect is my love,
And I in such a poverty of grace,
That I shall think it a most plenteous crop   100
To glean the broken ears after the man
That the main harvest reaps: lose now and then
A scatter'd smile, and that I'll live upon.

Phebe   Know'st thou the youth that spoke to me erewhile?

Silvius   Not very well, but I have met him oft,   [105-07]
And he hath bought the cottage and the bounds
That the old carlot once was master of.

Phebe   Think not I love him, though I ask for him;
'Tis but a peevish boy, yet he talks well;
But what care I for words? Yet words do well   110
When he that speaks them pleases those that hear:
It is a pretty youth, not very pretty,
But, sure, he's proud, and yet his pride becomes him;
He'll make a proper man: the best thing in him
Is his complexion: and faster than his tongue
Did make offence, his eye did heal it up:
He is not very tall, yet for his years he's tall:
His leg is but so so, and yet 'tis well:
There was a pretty redness in his lip,
A little riper, and more lusty red   120
Than that mix'd in his cheek; 'twas just the difference
Betwixt the constant red and mingled damask.

---

101   **glean:** gather corn left by the reapers
107   **carlot:** churl, peasant

John Jarvis as Silvius and Mary Haney as Phebe

There be some women, Silvius, had they mark'd him
In parcels as I did, would have gone near
To fall in love with him: but, for my part,
I love him not, nor hate him not; and yet
I have more cause to hate him than to love him,
For what had he to do to chide at me?
He said mine eyes were black, and my hair black,
And, now I am remember'd, scorn'd at me: 130
I marvel why I answer'd not again,
But that's all one: omittance is no quittance:
I'll write to him a very taunting letter,
And thou shalt bear it, wilt thou, Silvius?

Silvius   Phebe, with all my heart.

Phebe   I'll write it straight;
The matter's in my head, and in my heart,
I will be bitter with him, and passing short;
Go with me, Silvius.   *Exeunt*

Act Fourth

Scene 1

[Scene 24]

The forest
Enter Rosalind, Celia, and Jaques

Jaques   I prithee, pretty youth, let me be better acquainted
with thee.

Rosalind   They say you are a melancholy fellow.

Jaques   I am so; I do love it better than laughing.

Rosalind   Those that are in extremity of either are abominable
fellows, and betray themselves to every modern
censure, worse than drunkards.

Jaques   Why, 'tis good to be sad and say nothing.

Rosalind   Why then, 'tis good to be a post.

Jaques   I have neither the scholar's melancholy, which is   10
emulation; nor the musician's, which is fantastical;
nor the courtier's, which is proud; nor the soldier's,
which is ambitious; nor the lawyer's, which is
politic; nor the lady's, which is nice; nor the
lover's, which is all these: but it is a melancholy
of mine own, compounded of many simples, ex-
tracted from many objects, and indeed the sundry
contemplation of my travels, in which my often   [18]
rumination wraps me in a most humorous sadness.

Rosalind   A traveller! By my faith, you have great reason to   20
be sad: I fear you have sold your own lands, to see
other men's; then, to have seen much, and to have
nothing, is to have rich eyes, and poor hands.

Jaques	Yes, I have gain'd my experience.
Rosalind	And your experience makes you sad: I had rather have a fool to make me merry than experience to make me sad, and to travel for it too!

Enter Orlando

Orlando	Good-day, and happiness, dear Rosalind!
Jaques	Nay, then, God buy you, an you talk in blank verse.
Rosalind	Farewell, Monsieur Traveller: look you lisp, and wear strange suits; disable all the benefits of your own country; be out of love with your nativity, and almost chide God for making you that countenance you are; or I will scarce think you have swam in a gondola. *(Exit Jaques.)* Why, how now, Orlando, where have you been all this while? You a lover! An you serve me such another trick, never come in my sight more.
Orlando	My fair Rosalind, I come within an hour of my promise.
Rosalind	Break an hour's promise in love! He that will divide a minute into a thousand parts, and break but a part of the thousandth part of a minute in the affairs of love, it may be said of him that Cupid hath clapped him o' the shoulder, but I'll warrant him heart-whole.
Orlando	Pardon me, dear Rosalind.
Rosalind	Nay, an you be so tardy, come no more in my sight, I had as lief be woo'd of a snail.
Orlando	Of a snail?
Rosalind	Ay, of a snail: for though he comes slowly, he carries his house on his head; a better jointure, I think, than you make a woman: besides, he brings his destiny with him.
Orlando	What's that?
Rosalind	Why, horns: which such as you are fain to be beholding to your wives for: but he comes armed in his fortune, and prevents the slander of his wife.
Orlando	Virtue is no horn-maker: and my Rosalind is virtuous.
Rosalind	And I am your Rosalind.

30
[31-36]
40
50
60

31 **lisp:** speak with a foreign accent
32 **disable:** belittle

Celia	It pleases him to call you so; but he hath a Rosalind of a better leer than you.
Rosalind	Come, woo me, woo me: for now I am in a holiday humour, and like enough to consent. What would you say to me now, an I were your very, very Rosalind?
Orlando	I would kiss before I spoke.
Rosalind	Nay, you were better speak first, and when you were gravell'd, for lack of matter, you might take occasion to kiss: very good orators, when they are out, they will spit, and for lovers, lacking, God warrant us, matter, the cleanliest shift is to kiss.
Orlando	How if the kiss be denied?
Rosalind	Then she puts you to entreaty, and there begins new matter.
Orlando	Who could be out, being before his beloved mistress?
Rosalind	Marry, that should you, if I were your mistress, or I should think my honesty ranker than my wit.
Orlando	What, of my suit?
Rosalind	Not out of your apparel, and yet out of your suit. Am not I your Rosalind?
Orlando	I take some joy to say you are, because I would be talking of her.
Rosalind	Well, in her person, I say I will not have you.
Orlando	Then in mine own person, I die.
Rosalind	No, faith, die by attorney: the poor world is almost six thousand years old, and in all this time there was not any man died in his own person, videlicet, in a love-cause: Troilus had his brains dash'd out with a Grecian club, yet he did what he could to die before, and he is one of the patterns of love. Leander, he would have liv'd many a fair year though Hero had turn'd nun; if it had not been for a hot midsummer night, for, good youth, he went but forth to wash him in the Hellespont, and being taken with the cramp, was drown'd, and the foolish chroniclers of that age found it was 'Hero of Sestos.' But these are all lies, men have died from time to time, and worms have eaten them, but not for love.
Orlando	I would not have my right Rosalind of this mind, for I protest her frown might kill me.

70

[79-82]
80

[90]

100

---

71 **gravell'd:** at a loss
80 **honesty:** virtue
88 **by attorney:** by proxy
90 **videlicet:** namely

Rosalind	By this hand, it will not kill a fly. But come, now
	I will be your Rosalind in a more coming-on disposi-
	tion: and ask me what you will, I will grant it.
Orlando	Then love me, Rosalind.
Rosalind	Yes, faith, will I, Fridays and Saturdays, and all.
Orlando	And wilt thou have me?
Rosalind	Ay, and twenty such. 110
Orlando	What sayest thou?
Rosalind	Are you not good?
Orlando	I hope so.
Rosalind	Why then, can one desire too much of a good thing?
	Come, sister, you shall be the priest, and marry us:
	give me your hand, Orlando. What do you say,
	sister?
Orlando	Pray thee, marry us.
Celia	I cannot say the words.
Rosalind	You must begin, 'Will you, Orlando – 120
Celia	Go to. Will you, Orlando, have to wife this
	Rosalind?
Orlando	I will.
Rosalind	Ay, but when?
Orlando	Why now, as fast as she can marry us.
Rosalind	Then you must say 'I take thee, Rosalind, for
	wife.'
Orlando	I take thee, Rosalind, for wife.
Rosalind	I might ask you for your commission, but I do [129]
	take thee, Orlando, for my husband: there's a girl 130
	goes before the priest, and certainly a woman's
	thought runs before her actions.
Orlando	So do all thoughts, they are wing'd.
Rosalind	Now tell me how long you would have her, after
	you have possess'd her.
Orlando	For ever, and a day.
Rosalind	Say 'a day,' without the 'ever.' No, no, Orlando,
	men are April when they woo, December when they
	wed; maids are May when they are maids, but the
	sky changes when they are wives. I will be more 140
	jealous of thee than a Barbary cock-pigeon over his
	hen, more clamorous than a parrot against rain, more
	new-fangled than an ape, more giddy in my desires
	than a monkey: I will weep for nothing, like Diana [144]

---

129   **commission:** authority

The mock wedding vows:
Celia: "Will you, Orlando, have to wife this Rosalind?"

	in the fountain, and I will do that when you are dispos'd to be merry; I will laugh like a hyen, and that when thou art inclin'd to sleep.
Orlando	But will my Rosalind do so?
Rosalind	By my life, she will do as I do.
Orlando	O, but she is wise.
Rosalind	Or else she could not have the wit to do this: the wiser, the waywarder: make the doors upon a woman's wit, and it will out at the casement: shut that, and 'twill out at the key-hole: stop that, 'twill fly with the smoke out at the chimney.
Orlando	A man that had a wife with such a wit, he might say 'Wit, whither wilt?'
Rosalind	Nay, you might keep that check for it, till you met your wife's wit going to your neighbour's bed.
Orlando	And what wit could wit have, to excuse that.
Rosalind	Marry, to say she came to seek you there: you shall never take her without her answer, unless you take her without her tongue. O, that woman that cannot make her fault her husband's occasion, let her never nurse her child herself, for she will breed it like a fool!
Orlando	For these two hours, Rosalind, I will leave thee.
Rosalind	Alas, dear love, I cannot lack thee two hours.
Orlando	I must attend the Duke at dinner, by two o'clock I will be with thee again.
Rosalind	Ay, go your ways, go your ways: I knew what you would prove, my friends told me as much, and I thought no less: that flattering tongue of yours won me: 'tis but one cast away, and so, come, death! Two o'clock is your hour?
Orlando	Ay, sweet Rosalind.
Rosalind	By my troth, and in good earnest, and so God mend me, and by all pretty oaths that are not dangerous, if you break one jot of your promise, or come one minute behind your hour, I will think you the most pathetical break-promise, and the most hollow lover, and the most unworthy of her you call Rosalind, that may be chosen out of the gross band of the unfaithful: therefore beware my censure, and keep your promise.

150

160

170

180

152 **make:** bar

Orlando	With no less religion than if thou wert indeed my Rosalind: so adieu.
Rosalind	Well, Time is the old justice that examines all such offenders, and let Time try: adieu.

Exit Orlando

Celia	You have simply misus'd our sex in your loveprate: We must have your doublet and hose pluck'd over your head, and show the world what the bird hath done to her own nest.	190
Rosalind	O coz, coz, coz: my pretty little coz, that thou didst know how many fathom deep I am in love! But it cannot be sounded: my affection hath an unknown bottom, like the bay of Portugal.	
Celia	Or rather, bottomless, that as fast as you pour affection in, it runs out.	
Rosalind	No, that same wicked bastard of Venus, that was begot of thought, conceiv'd of spleen, and born of madness, that blind rascally boy, that abuses every one's eyes because his own are out, let him be judge, how deep I am in love: I'll tell thee, Aliena, I cannot be out of the sight of Orlando: I'll go find a shadow, and sigh till he come.	200
Celia	And I'll sleep. *Exeunt*	

---

190 **simply misus'd:** completely disgraced
200 **bastard of Venus:** Cupid
201 **spleen:** caprice

Scene 2

The forest
Enter Jaques and Lords, foresters

Jaques   Which is he that killed the deer?

A Lord   Sir, it was I.

Jaques   Let's present him to the Duke like a Roman con-
queror, and it would do well to set the deer's horns
upon his head, for a branch of victory. Have you
no song, forester, for this purpose?

A Lord   Yes, sir.

Jaques   Sing it: 'tis no matter how it be in tune, so it make
noise enough.

SONG

What shall he have that kill'd the deer?   10
His leather skin, and horns to wear:
Then sing him home: the rest shall bear
  This burden.
Take thou no scorn to wear the horn,
It was a crest ere thou wast born,
  Thy father's father wore it,
  And thy father bore it:
The horn, the horn, the lusty horn,
Is not a thing to laugh to scorn.   *Exeunt*

JAQUES.

Scene 3

The forest
Enter Rosalind and Celia

Rosalind	How say you now, is it not past two o'clock? And here much Orlando!
Celia	I warrant you, with pure love, and troubled brain, he hath ta'en his bow and arrows, and is gone forth to sleep: look, who comes here.

Enter Silvius

Silvius   My errand is to you, fair youth;
My gentle Phebe did bid me give you this:
I know not the contents, but, as I guess
By the stern brow, and waspish action
Which she did use, as she was writing of it,   10
It bears an angry tenour; pardon me,
I am but as a guiltless messenger.

Rosalind   Patience herself would startle at this letter,
And play the swaggerer; bear this, bear all.
She says I am not fair, that I lack manners,
She calls me proud, and that she could not love me
Were man as rare as phoenix: 'od's my will,
Her love is not the hare that I do hunt,
Why writes she so to me? Well, shepherd, well,
This is a letter of your own device.   20

Silvius   No, I protest, I know not the contents.
Phebe did write it.

Rosalind   Come, come, you are a fool,
And turn'd into the extremity of love.
I saw her hand, she has a leathern hand,
A freestone-colour'd hand, I verily did think
That her old gloves were on, but 'twas her hands:
She has a huswife's hand, but that's no matter:
I say she never did invent this letter,
This is a man's invention, and his hand.

Silvius   Sure, it is hers.   30

Rosalind   Why, 'tis a boisterous and a cruel style,
A style for challengers: why, she defies me,

---

25 **freestone-colour'd:** brownish-yellow, like a brick

	Like Turk to Christian: women's gentle brain
	Could not drop forth such giant rude invention,
	Such Ethiop words, blacker in their effect
	Than in their countenance. Will you hear the letter?
Silvius	So please you, for I never heard it yet;
	Yet heard too much of Phebe's cruelty.
Rosalind	She Phebes me; mark how the tyrant writes:

Silvius	*(reads)* Art thou god to shepherd turn'd,
	That a maiden's heart hath burn'd?
	Can a woman rail thus?
Silvius	Call you this railing?
Rosalind	*(reads)*

40

[44-49]

       Why, thy godhead laid apart,
       Warr'st thou with a woman's heart?
Did you ever hear such railing?
       Whiles the eye of man did woo me,
       That could do no vengeance to me.
Meaning me a beast.
       If the scorn of your bright eyne   50
       Have power to raise such love in mine,
       Alack, in me, what strange effect
       Would they work in mild aspect?
       Whiles you chid me, I did love
       How then might your prayers move?
       He that brings this love to thee,
       Little knows this love in me:
       And by him seal up thy mind,
       Whether that thy youth and kind
       Will the faithful offer take   60
       Of me, and all that I can make,
       Or else by him my love deny,
       And then I'll study how to die.

Silvius	Call you this chiding?
Celia	Alas, poor shepherd!
Rosalind	Do you pity him? No, he deserves no pity: wilt
	thou love such a woman? What, to make thee an
	instrument, and play false strains upon thee? Not to
	be endur'd! Well, go your way to her; for I see
	love hath made thee a tame snake, and say this to 70
	her; that if she love me, I charge her to love thee:
	if she will not, I will never have her, unless thou

---

50 **eyne:** eyes
53 **aspect:** look; phase (in astrological sense)

entreat for her: if you be a true lover, hence, and not
a word; for here comes more company.

Exit Silvius

Enter Oliver   [Scene 27]

Oliver   Good morrow, fair ones: pray you, if you know,
                Where in the purlieus of this forest stands
                A sheep-cote, fenc'd about with olive-trees?   [77]
Celia   West of this place, down in the neighbour bottom, [78]
                The rank of osiers, by the murmuring stream
                Left on your right hand, brings you to the place. 80
                But at this hour the house doth keep itself,
                There's none within.
Oliver   If that an eye may profit by a tongue,
                Then should I know you by description,
                Such garments, and such years: 'The boy is fair,
                Of female favour, and bestows himself   [86-88]
                Like a ripe forester: the woman low
                And browner than her brother': are not you
                The owner of the house I did enquire for?
Celia   It is no boast, being ask'd, to say we are.   90
Oliver   Orlando doth commend him to you both,
                And to that youth he calls his Rosalind
                He sends this bloody napkin; are you he?
Rosalind   I am: what must we understand by this?
Oliver   Some of my shame, if you will know of me
                What man I am, and how, and why, and where
                This handkercher was stain'd.
Celia   I pray you tell it.
Oliver   When last the young Orlando parted from you,
                He left a promise to return again
                Within an hour, and pacing through the forest,   [100]
                Chewing the food of sweet and bitter fancy,
                Lo, what befel! He threw his eye aside,   [102]
                And mark what object did present itself
                Under an old oak, whose boughs were moss'd with age
                And high top, bald with dry antiquity:
                A wretched ragged man, o'ergrown with hair,
                Lay sleeping on his back; about his neck
                A green and gilded snake had wreath'd itself,

76 **purlieus:** borders
79 **osiers:** willows

Rosalind, Oliver, and Celia

	Who with her head nimble in threats approach'd	
	The opening of his mouth: but suddenly	110
	Seeing Orlando, it unlink'd itself,	
	And with indented glides did slip away	
	Into a bush, under which bush's shade	
	A lioness, with udders all drawn dry,	
	Lay couching head on ground, with catlike watch	
	When that the sleeping man should stir; for 'tis	
	The royal disposition of that beast	
	To prey on nothing that doth seem as dead:	
	This seen, Orlando did approach the man,	
	And found it was his brother, his elder brother.	120

Celia O, I have heard him speak of that same brother;
And he did render him the most unnatural
That liv'd amongst men.

Oliver   And well he might so do,
For well I know he was unnatural.

Rosalind But to Orlando: did he leave him there,
Food to the suck'd and hungry lioness?

Oliver Twice did he turn his back, and purpos'd so:
But kindness, nobler ever than revenge,
And nature stronger than his just occasion,
Made him give battle to the lioness,   130
Who quickly fell before him, in which hurtling
From miserable slumber I awak'd.

Celia Are you his brother?

Rosalind   Was 't you he rescu'd?

Celia Was 't you that did so oft contrive to kill him?

Oliver 'Twas I: but 'tis not I: I do not shame
To tell you what I was, since my conversion
So sweetly tastes, being the thing I am.

Rosalind But for the bloody napkin?

Oliver   By and by: [138]
When from the first to last betwixt us two
Tears our recountments had most kindly bath'd,   140
As how I came into that desert place;
In brief, he led me to the gentle Duke,
Who gave me fresh array, and entertainment,
Committing me unto my brother's love,
Who led me instantly unto his cave,

---

112 **indented:** undulating

There stripp'd himself, and here upon his arm
The lioness had torn some flesh away,
Which all this while had bled; and now he fainted,
And cried in fainting upon Rosalind.
Brief, I recover'd him, bound up his wound,   150
And after some small space, being strong at heart,
He sent me hither, stranger as I am,
To tell this story, that you might excuse
His broken promise, and to give this napkin
Dyed in his blood, unto the shepherd youth,
That he in sport doth call his Rosalind.

Rosalind swoons

Celia	Why, how now, Ganymede, sweet Ganymede?
Oliver	Many will swoon when they do look on blood.
Celia	There is more in it. Cousin – Ganymede!
Oliver	Look, he recovers. 160
Rosalind	I would I were at home.
Celia	We'll lead you thither.
	I pray you, will you take him by the arm?
Oliver	Be of good cheer, youth: you a man? You lack a man's heart.
Rosalind	I do so, I confess it. Ah, sirrah, a body would think this was well counterfeited, I pray you, tell your brother how well I counterfeited. Heigh-ho!
Oliver	This was not counterfeit, there is too great testimony in your complexion that it was a passion of earnest. 170
Rosalind	Counterfeit, I assure you.
Oliver	Well then, take a good heart, and counterfeit to be a man.
Rosalind	So I do: but, i' faith, I should have been a woman by right.
Celia	Come, you look paler and paler: pray you, draw homewards: good sir, go with us.
Oliver	That will I: for I must bear answer back How you excuse my brother, Rosalind.
Rosalind	I shall devise something: but I pray you commend my counterfeiting to him. Will you go? *Exeunt* 180

Act·Fifth

Scene 1

The forest
Enter Touchstone and Audrey

Touchstone	We shall find a time, Audrey; patience, gentle Audrey.
Audrey	Faith, the priest was good enough, for all the old gentleman's saying.
Touchstone	A most wicked Sir Oliver, Audrey, a most vile Martext. But Audrey, there is a youth here in the forest lays claim to you.
Audrey	Ay, I know who 'tis: he hath no interest in me in the world: here comes the man you mean.
Touchstone	It is meat and drink to me to see a clown: by my troth, we that have good wits have much to answer for; we shall be flouting; we cannot hold.

10

Enter William

William	Good ev'n, Audrey.
Audrey	God ye good ev'n, William.
William	And good ev'n to you, sir.
Touchstone	Good ev'n, gentle friend. Cover thy head, cover thy head; nay, prithee, be cover'd. How old are you, friend?
William	Five and twenty, sir.
Touchstone	A ripe age. Is thy name William?
William	William, sir.
Touchstone	A fair name. Wast born i' the forest here?
William	Ay, sir, I thank God.

20

---

12 **flouting:** jeering, teasing

Touchstone	'Thank God;' a good answer. Art rich?
William	Faith, sir, so so.
Touchstone	'So so' is good, very good, very excellent good;
	and yet it is not, it is but so so. Art thou wise?
William	Ay, sir, I have a pretty wit.
Touchstone	Why, thou say'st well. I do now remember a

Touchstone saying, 'The fool doth think he is wise, but the wise 30
man knows himself to be a fool.' The heathen [31-35]
philosopher, when he had a desire to eat a grape,
would open his lips when he put it into his mouth,
meaning thereby, that grapes were made to eat, and
lips to open. You do love this maid?

William I do, sir.

Touchstone Give me your hand. Art thou learned?

William No, sir.

Touchstone Then learn this of me: to have, is to have. For
it is a figure in rhetoric, that drink being pour'd out 40
of a cup into a glass, by filling the one, doth empty
the other. For all your writers do consent, that
ipse is he: now you are not *ipse*, for I am he.

William Which he, sir?

Touchstone He, sir, that must marry this woman: therefore,
you clown, abandon, – which is in the vulgar leave
– the society, – which in the boorish is company, –
of this female, – which in the common is woman:
which together, is, abandon the society of this
female, or, clown, thou perishest: or, to thy better 50
understanding, diest; or, to wit, I kill thee, make
thee away, translate life into death, thy liberty
into bondage: I will deal in poison with thee, or
in bastinado, or in steel: I will bandy with thee in
faction, I will o'er-run thee with policy; I will kill
thee a hundred and fifty ways, therefore tremble,
and depart.

Audrey Do, good William.

William God rest you merry, sir.   *Exit*

Enter Corin

Corin Our master and mistress seeks you: come away, away! 60

Touchstone Trip, Audrey! Trip, Audrey! I attend, I attend. *Exeunt*

---

54 **bastinado:** beating with a cudgel

Scene 2

The forest
Enter Orlando and Oliver

Orlando	Is 't possible that on so little acquaintance you should like her? That, but seeing, you should love her? And loving woo? And wooing, she should grant? And will you persever to enjoy her?
Oliver	Neither call the giddiness of it in question; the poverty of her, the small acquaintance, my sudden wooing, nor sudden consenting: but say with me, I love Aliena; say with her, that she loves me; consent with both, that we may enjoy each other: it shall be to your good; for my father's house, and all the revenue that was old Sir Rowland's, will I estate upon you, and here live and die a shepherd.
Orlando	You have my consent. Let your wedding be to-morrow: thither will I invite the Duke, and all 's contented followers. Go you, and prepare Aliena; for look you, here comes my Rosalind.

Enter Rosalind

Rosalind	God save you, brother.
Oliver	And you, fair sister. *Exit*
Rosalind	O, my dear Orlando, how it grieves me to see thee wear thy heart in a scarf!
Orlando	It is my arm.
Rosalind	I thought thy heart had been wounded with the claws of a lion.
Orlando	Wounded it is, but with the eyes of a lady.
Rosalind	Did your brother tell you how I counterfeited to swoon, when he show'd me your handkercher?
Orlando	Ay, and greater wonders than that.
Rosalind	O, I know where you are: nay, 'tis true: there was never any thing so sudden, but the fight of two rams, and Cæsar's thrasonical brag of 'I came, saw, and overcame:' for your brother, and my

10

20

[27]

30

---

31   **thrasonical:** boastful

sister, no sooner met, but they look'd; no sooner
look'd, but they lov'd; no sooner lov'd, but they
sigh'd; no sooner sigh'd but they ask'd one another
the reason; no sooner knew the reason, but they
sought the remedy: and in these degrees, have they
made a pair of stairs to marriage, which they will
climb incontinent, or else be incontinent before
marriage: they are in the very wrath of love and   40
they will together. Clubs cannot part them.

Orlando   They shall be married to-morrow: and I will bid
the Duke to the nuptial. But, O, how bitter a
thing it is, to look into happiness through another
man's eyes! By so much the more shall I to-
morrow be at the height of heart-heaviness, by
how much I shall think my brother happy, in
having what he wishes for.

Rosalind   Why, then, to-morrow I cannot serve your turn
for Rosalind?   50

Orlando   I can live no longer by thinking.

Rosalind   I will weary you then no longer with idle talking.
Know of me then, for now I speak to some purpose,
that I know you are a gentleman of good conceit: [54-60]
I speak not this that you should bear a good opinion
of my knowledge: insomuch, I say, I know you
are; neither do I labour for a greater esteem than
may in some little measure draw a belief from you,
to do yourself good, and not to grace me. Believe
then, if you please, that I can do strange things: 60
I have, since I was three year old, convers'd with
a magician, most profound in his art, and yet not
damnable. If you do love Rosalind so near the   [63]
heart as your gesture cries it out; when your
brother marries Aliena, shall you marry her. I
know into what straits of fortune she is driven,
and it is not impossible to me, if it appear not
inconvenient to you, to set her before your eyes
to-morrow, human as she is, and without any danger.

Orlando   Speak'st thou in sober meanings?   70

Rosalind   By my life, I do, which I tender dearly, though   [71]
I say I am a magician. Therefore put you in your

---

54 **conceit:** understanding
61 **convers'd:** studied

best array, bid your friends; for if you will be
married to-morrow, you shall; and to Rosalind,
if you will.

Enter Silvius and Phebe

	Look, here comes a lover of mine, and a lover of hers.	
Phebe	Youth, you have done me much ungentleness,	
	To show the letter that I writ to you.	
Rosalind	I care not if I have: it is my study	
	To seem despiteful and ungentle to you:	80
	You are there followed by a faithful shepherd,	
	Look upon him, love him; he worships you.	
Phebe	Good shepherd, tell this youth what 'tis to love.	
Silvius	It is to be all made of sighs and tears,	
	And so am I for Phebe.	
Phebe	And I for Ganymede.	
Orlando	And I for Rosalind.	
Rosalind	And I for no woman.	
Silvius	It is to be all made of faith and service,	
	And so am I for Phebe.	90
Phebe	And I for Ganymede.	
Orlando	And I for Rosalind.	
Rosalind	And I for no woman.	
Silvius	It is to be all made of fantasy,	
	All made of passion, and all made of wishes,	
	All adoration, duty, and observance,	
	All humbleness, all patience, and impatience,	
	All purity, all trial, all observance;	
	And so am I for Phebe.	
Phebe	And so am I for Ganymede.	100
Orlando	And so am I for Rosalind.	
Rosalind	And so am I for no woman.	
Phebe	If this be so, why blame you me to love you?	
Silvius	If this be so, why blame you me to love you?	
Orlando	If this be so, why blame you me to love you?	
Rosalind	Who do you speak to, 'Why blame you me to love you?'	
Orlando	To her that is not here, nor doth not hear.	
Rosalind	Pray you, no more of this, 'tis like the howling of	
	Irish wolves against the moon. *(To Silvius)* I will help	110
	you, if I can. *(To Phebe)* I would love you, if I could.	

Touchstone: "Tomorrow is a joyful day."

To-morrow meet me all together. *(To Phebe)* I will
marry you, if ever I marry woman, and I'll be
married to-morrow. *(To Orlando)* I will satisfy you, if
ever I satisfied man, and you shall be married to-
morrow. *(To Silvius)* I will content you, if what pleases
you contents you, and you shall be married to-
morrow. *(To Orlando)* As you love Rosalind, meet.
(To Silvius) As you love Phebe, meet. And as I love no
woman, I'll meet. So, fare you well: I have left   120
you commands.

Silvius   I'll not fail, if I live.
Phebe   Nor I.
Orlando   Nor I.   *Exeunt*

Scene 3

The forest
Enter Touchstone and Audrey

Touchstone   To-morrow is the joyful day, Audrey, to-morrow
                 will we be married.
Audrey   I do desire it with all my heart; and I hope it is
                 no dishonest desire, to desire to be a woman of the
                 world? Here come two of the banish'd Duke's
                 pages.

Enter two Pages

First Page   Well met, honest gentleman.
Touchstone   By my troth, well met: come, sit, sit, and a song.
Second Page We are for you, sit i' the middle.
First Page   Shall we clap into 't roundly, without hawk-   10
                 ing or spitting, or saying we are hoarse, which are
                 the only prologues to a bad voice?
Second Page I' faith, i' faith, and both in a tune like two
                 gipsies on a horse.

SONG

It was a lover, and his lass,
　　With a hey, and a ho, and a hey nonino,
That o'er the green corn-field did pass,
　　In the spring time, the only pretty ring time,
When birds do sing, hey ding a ding, ding:
　　Sweet lovers love the spring.　　　　　　　　　　　　　　20

Between the acres of the rye,
　　With a hey, and a ho, and a hey nonino,
These pretty country folks would lie,
　　In spring time, &c.

This carol they began that hour,
　　With a hey, and a ho, and a hey nonino,
How that a life was but a flower
　　In spring time, &c.

And therefore take the present time,
　　With a hey, and a ho, and a hey nonino;　　　　　　　30
For love is crowned with the prime
　　In spring time, &c.

Touchstone　　Truly, young gentlemen, though there was no great
matter in the ditty, yet the note was very untuneable.

First Page　　You are deceiv'd, sir, we kept time, we lost
not our time.

Touchstone　　By my troth, yes; I count it but time lost to hear
such a foolish song. God buy you, and God mend
your voices! Come, Audrey.　　　　　　　　　*Exeunt*

Scene 4

The forest
Enter Duke Senior, Amiens, Jaques, Orlando, Oliver,
and Celia

Duke Senior	Dost thou believe, Orlando, that the boy
	Can do all this that he hath promised?
Orlando	I sometimes do believe, and sometimes do not,
	As those that fear they hope, and know they fear.

Enter Rosalind, Silvius, and Phebe

Rosalind	Patience once more, whiles our compact is urg'd:	
	You say, if I bring in your Rosalind,	
	You will bestow her on Orlando here?	
Duke Senior	That would I, had I kingdoms to give with her.	
Rosalind	And you say you will have her, when I bring her.	
Orlando	That would I, were I of all kingdoms king.	10
Rosalind	You say, you'll marry me, if I be willing?	
Phebe	That will I, should I die the hour after.	
Rosalind	But if you do refuse to marry me,	
	You'll give yourself to this most faithful shepherd?	
Phebe	So is the bargain.	
Rosalind	You say that you'll have Phebe if she will?	
Silvius	Though to have her and death were both one thing.	
Rosalind	I have promis'd to make all this matter even.	
	Keep you your word, O Duke, to give your daughter,	
	And yours, Orlando, to receive his daughter.	20
	Keep you your word, Phebe, that you'll marry me,	
	Or else refusing me to wed this shepherd.	
	Keep your word, Silvius, that you'll marry her	
	If she refuse me, and from hence I go	
	To make these doubts all even.	

Exeunt Rosalind and Celia

Duke Senior	I do remember in this shepherd boy	
	Some lively touches of my daughter's favour.	
Orlando	My lord, the first time that I ever saw him,	
	Methought he was a brother to your daughter:	
	But, my good lord, this boy is forest-born,	30
	And hath been tutor'd in the rudiments	

Of many desperate studies, by his uncle,
Whom he reports to be a great magician.
Obscured in the circle of this forest.

Enter Touchstone and Audrey

Jaques	There is sure another flood toward, and these couples are coming to the ark. Here comes a pair of very strange beasts, which in all tongues are called fools.
Touchstone	Salutation and greeting to you all!
Jaques	Good my lord, bid him welcome: this is the motley-minded gentleman, that I have so often met in the forest: he hath been a courtier, he swears.
Touchstone	If any man doubt that, let him put me to my purgation, I have trod a measure, I have flatter'd a lady, I have been politic with my friend, smooth with mine enemy, I have undone three tailors, I have had four quarrels, and like to have fought one.
Jaques	And how was that ta'en up?
Touchstone	Faith, we met, and found the quarrel was upon the seventh cause.
Jaques	How seventh cause? Good my lord, like this fellow.
Duke Senior	I like him very well.
Touchstone	God 'ild you, sir, I desire you of the like. I press in here, sir, amongst the rest of the country copulatives, to swear, and to forswear, according as marriage binds and blood breaks: a poor virgin, sir, an ill-favour'd thing, sir, but mine own, a poor humour of mine, sir, to take that that no man else will: rich honesty dwells like a miser, sir, in a poor house, as your pearl in your foul oyster.
Duke Senior	By my faith, he is very swift, and sententious.
Touchstone	According to the fool's bolt, sir, and such dulcet diseases.
Jaques	But for the seventh cause. How did you find the quarrel on the seventh cause?
Touchstone	Upon a lie, seven times removed: – bear your body more seeming, Audrey: – as thus, sir. I did

40

[46]

50

60

[63-64]

---

43 **put me to my purgation:** let me clear myself
57 **blood breaks:** passion wanes

dislike the cut of a certain courtier's beard: he sent [69]
me word, if I said his beard was not cut well, he 70
was in the mind it was: this is call'd the retort
courteous. If I sent him word again, 'it was not
well cut,' he would send me word he cut it to please
himself: this is call'd the quip modest. If again,
'it was not well cut,' he disabled my judgement:
this is call'd the reply churlish. If again, 'it was
not well cut,' he would answer I spake not true:
this is call'd the reproof valiant. If again, 'it was
not well cut,' he would say, I lie: this is call'd the
countercheck quarrelsome: and so to lie circum- 80
stantial, and the lie direct.

Jaques And how oft did you say his beard was not well
cut?

Touchstone I durst go no further than the Lie Circumstantial:
nor he durst not give me the Lie Direct: and so
we measur'd swords, and parted.

Jaques Can you nominate in order now, the degrees of the
lie?

Touchstone O sir, we quarrel in print, by the book: as you
have books for good manners: I will name you 90
the degrees. The first, the Retort courteous: the
second, the Quip modest: the third, the Reply
churlish: the fourth, the Reproof valiant; the fifth,
the Countercheck quarrelsome: the sixth, the Lie
with circumstance: the seventh, the Lie direct: all
these you may avoid but the Lie direct: and you
may avoid that too, with an If. I knew when seven
justices could not take up a quarrel, but when the
parties were met themselves, one of them thought
but of an If; as, 'If you said so, then I said 100
so:' and they shook hands, and swore brothers.
Your If is the only peace-maker: much virtue
in If.

Jaques Is not this a rare fellow, my lord? He's as good at
any thing, and yet a fool.

Duke Senior He uses his folly like a stalking-horse, and under the
presentation of that he shoots his wit.

Enter Hymen, Rosalind, and Celia
Still Music

Hymen Then is there mirth in heaven, [108]
When earthly things made even
   Atone together, 110
Good Duke, receive thy daughter:
Hymen from heaven brought her,
   Yea, brought her hither,
That thou mightst join his hand with his
Whose heart within his bosom is.

Rosalind To you I give myself, for I am yours.
To you I give myself, for I am yours.

Duke Senior If there be truth in sight, you are my daughter.
Orlando If there be truth in sight, you are my Rosalind.
Phebe If sight and shape be true, 120
Why then, my love adieu!

Rosalind I'll have no father, if you be not he:
I'll have no husband, if you be not he:
Nor ne'er wed woman, if you be not she.

Hymen Peace, ho! I bar confusion:
'Tis I must make conclusion
   Of these most strange events:
Here's eight that must take hands.
To join in Hymen's bands.
   If truth holds true contents. 130
You and you, no cross shall part:
You and you, are heart in heart:
You, to his love must accord,
Or have a woman to your lord:
You and you, are sure together,
As the winter to foul weather.
Whiles a wedlock-hymn we sing,
Feed yourselves with questioning:
That reason wonder may diminish,
How thus we met, and these things finish. 140

Rosalind and Orlando are wed in the Forest of Arden

SONG

Wedding is great Juno's crown,
   O blessed bond of board and bed!
'Tis Hymen peoples every town,
   High wedlock then be honoured:
Honour, high honour and renown,
To Hymen, god of every town!

Duke Senior   O my dear niece, welcome thou art to me,
             Even daughter welcome, in no less degree.
Phebe   I will not eat my word, now thou art mine;
             Thy faith my fancy to thee doth combine.   150

Enter Jaques de Boys

de Boys   Let me have audience for a word or two:
             I am the second son of old Sir Rowland,
That bring these tidings to this fair assembly.
Duke Frederick, hearing how that every day
Men of great worth resorted to this forest,
Address'd a mighty power, which were on foot
In his own conduct, purposely to take
His brother here, and put him to the sword:
And to the skirts of this wild wood he came;
Where, meeting with an old religious man,   160
After some question with him, was converted
Both from his enterprise, and from the world;
His crown bequeathing to his banish'd brother,
And all their lands restor'd to them again
That were with him exil'd. This to be true,
I do engage my life.
Duke Senior   Welcome, young man:

Thou offer'st fairly to thy brothers' wedding:
To one of his lands withheld, and to the other
A land itself at large, a potent dukedom.
First, in this forest, let us do those ends   170
That here were well begun, and well begot:
And after, every of this happy number
That have endur'd shrewd days and nights with us,
Shall share the good of our returned fortune,
According to the measure of their states.
Meantime, forget this new-fall'n dignity,

	And fall into our rustic revelry.	
	Play, music, and you brides and bridegrooms all,	
	With measure heap'd in joy, to the measures fall.	
Jaques	Sir, by your patience: if I heard you rightly,	180
	The Duke hath put on a religious life,	
	And thrown into neglect the pompous court.	
de Boys	He hath.	
Jaques	To him will I: out of these convertites	
	There is much matter to be heard and learn'd.	
	(to Duke Senior) You to your former honour I bequeath:	
	Your patience, and your virtue, well deserves it.	
	(to Orlando) You to a love, that your true faith doth merit.	
	(to Oliver) You to your land, and love, and great allies.	
	(to Silvius) You to a long, and well-deserved bed.	190
	(to Touchstone) And you to wrangling, for thy loving voyage	
	Is but for two months victuall'd. So, to your	
	pleasures:	
	I am for other than dancing measures.	
Duke Senior	Stay, Jaques, stay.	
Jaques	To see no pastime I: what you would have	
	I'll stay to know at your abandon'd cave. *Exit*	
Duke Senior	Proceed, proceed: we'll begin these rites,	
	As we do trust, they'll end in true delights.	
	Exeunt all except Rosalind	

Epilogue

Rosalind   It is not the fashion to see the lady the epilogue:
but it is no more unhandsome than to see the lord
the prologue. If it be true, that good wine needs   [3-4]
no bush, 'tis true, that a good play needs no epilogue.
Yet to good wine they do use good bushes: and
good plays prove the better by the help of good
epilogues. What a case am I in then, that am
neither a good epilogue, nor cannot insinuate with
you in the behalf of a good play? I am not fur-
nish'd like a beggar, therefore to beg will not become   10
me. My way is to conjure you, and I'll begin with
the women. I charge you, O women, for the love
you bear to men, to like as much of this play as
please you: and I charge you, O men, for the love
you bear to women, – as I perceive by your simper-
ing, none of you hates them, – that between you, and
the women, the play may please. If I were a woman,   [17]
I would kiss as many of you as had beards that
pleas'd me, complexions that lik'd me, and breaths
that I defied not: and, I am sure, as many as have   20
good beards, or good faces, or sweet breaths, will,
for my kind offer, when I make curtsy, bid me
farewell.   *Exit*

ROSOLIND. WEDDING.

Stratford Festival Edition Emendations

In the 1983 Stratford Festival Production of *As You Like It*, the following changes were made in the text for various reasons. Occasionally a new word was interjected in order to complement the action of a scene, or an obscure word was changed to a more accessible equivalent. In both cases, anachronism was avoided by using a word that would have been in use in Shakespeare's time.

Often entire lines were cut. Although their meaning was clear to the actor or to someone reading the words on the page with the aid of a glossary, it was found that certain opaque references interfered with the action of the play.

Some of the more difficult lines spoken in the play have been paraphrased below as an aid to readers.

Although such liberties may startle the purist, they ultimately lead to a greater enjoyment of the play on the part of the general audience.

Act I / Scene 1

line 2:

> "but poor a" was changed to "paltry."

lines 11 – 13:

> "For, besides . . . hired": The horses are broken in by well-paid trainers. In the 1983 Stratford Festival production of *As You Like It*, these lines were cut in order to expedite the action of the play.

line 20:

> *mines* was changed to *undermines*.

line 21:

> *my education* was changed to *this education*.

line 35:

> "be naught awhile" was changed to "be out of my sight."

lines 48 – 50:

"albeit ... reverence": I admit that, being first born you automatically deserve our father's respect, or, what belongs to our father. These lines were cut to expedite the action of the play.

lines 52 – 53:

stage direction: In the 1983 SF production, Oliver threatened Orlando and Orlando grabbed Oliver by the throat, knocking him to the ground.

lines 58 – 62:

"Wert thou ... at accord": These lines were cut in order to expedite the action of the play.

line 63:

I say was cut.

line 84:

physic was changed to *cure.*

line 85:

Holla was cut.

lines 89 – 90:

"at the ... to you" was changed to "My Lord."

line 91:

in was cut.

line 104 – 07:

"for the ... behind her": These lines were cut to expedite the action of the play.

lines 113 – 14:

"they say ... and fleet": This passage was changed to read: "Robin Hood of England, fleeting the time carelessly ... etc."

lines 124 – 25:

"For your ... come in": These lines were cut.

line 128:

intendment was changed to *intention.*

brook was changed to *endure.*

lines 129 – 30:

"in that ... my will": These lines were cut.

lines 146 – 50:

"for I assure ... and wonder": These lines were cut to expedite the action of the play.

line 164 – 65:

"Nothing ... go about": These lines were cut to expedite the action of the play.

Act I / *Scene 2*

line 30:

> *Fortune*: As defined in the OED: "Chance, hap, or luck regarded as a cause of events and changes in men's affairs. Often personified as a goddess, having for emblem a wheel, betokening vicissitude (the uncertain changing or mutability of something)."

line 40:

> *Nature*: As defined in the OED: "The creative and regulative physical power which is conceived of as operating in the physical world and as the immediate cause of all phenomena ... personified as a female being."

lines 46 – 53:

> "Indeed ... whetstone of the wits": This fast wordplay on the various properties of Nature and Fortune would have had enormous appeal to the Elizabethan audience; but in the 1983 SF production of *As You Like It* these lines were cut to expedite the action of the play.

line 58:

> In the 1983 SF production of the play, Rosalind repeated the oath "by your honour" before saying her line to clarify which "oath" she was talking about.

lines 60, 62, 74:

> *pancakes* was changed to *meat pies*.

lines 78 – 80:

> "My father's love ... days": In the Folio Rosalind says this line, but the generally accepted emendation gives this line to Celia, as in the 1983 SF production of *As You Like It*.

line 86:

> "the Beu": This unique spelling of Le Beau is preserved from the Folio, as a possible mimickry of Le Beau's affected manner of speech.

line 99:

> "thy old smell": Rosalind makes a pun on *rank*, meaning both office of employment and offensive smell.

lines 113 – 14:

> "With bills ... these presents": The "bills" would be proclamations, as were sometimes worn on the back, slung from the neck. "presents" is a possible pun on Le Beau's "presence," if, as some suggest, Le Beau's affected speech has reminded Rosalind of legal jargon (presents, being legal documents). Dr. Johnson said: "I know not well what to determine." In the 1983 SF production of the play, these lines were cut to expedite the action.

Prop builder Guy Nokes welding metal pipes to form trees.

line 258:

"But yet ... daughter": To see Shakespeare's inconsistency in the matter of Rosalind's height, see Act I/*Scene 3*, line 111 and Act IV/*Scene 3*, lines 86-88.

Act I / *Scene 3*

lines 22-24:

"You will ... service": Celia keeps up the wrestling metaphor. Though Rosalind lost in the first round, she will try again. These lines were cut.

lines 35-36:

"Look ... anger": In the 1983 Stratford production Duke Frederick entered from the centre balcony, and it was impossible for Rosalind and Celia to see his approach. Therefore, these lines were cut, and the two women were surprised by his entrance.

lines 45 – 46:

"If that ... dear uncle": These lines were cut.

line 71:

Juno's swans: It was Venus in fact to whom swans were sacred. Shakespeare's "mistake" has never been emended.

line 111:

"Because ... tall": As the actress playing Rosalind in the 1983 Stratford production was shorter than the actress playing Celia, this line was cut.

Act II / *Scene 1*

lines 13 – 14:

"the toad ... head": In the words of Dr. Johnson: "It was the current opinion in Shakespeare's time, that in the head of an old toad was to be found a stone, or pearl to which great virtues were ascribed. This stone has been often sought, but nothing has been found more than accidental, or perhaps morbid indurations of the skull."

lines 49 – 52:

"then, being ... company": These lines were cut to expedite the action of the scene.

lines 55 – 57:

"Sweep on ... there": This invective of Jaques compares the herd of deer which are racing by (ignorant of the dead deer on the bank) to the "greasy citizens" of the city who would likewise ignore the "broken bankrupt."

Act II / *Scene 2*

line 8:

roynish was changed to *churlish*.

line 17:

that gallant was changed to *Orlando* for clarity.

Act II / *Scene 3*

lines 2 – 4:

"O my ... Rowland": These lines were cut to expedite the action of the scene.

lines 5 – 6:

"Why are you ... and valiant?": These lines were cut to expedite the action of the scene.

lines 12 – 13:

"No more ... to you": These lines were cut.

lines 19 – 21:

"no, no ... his father": These lines were cut.

line 47 – 52:

"yet I am ... Therefore": These lines were cut.

Act II / *Scene 4*

lines 10 – 11:

"yet I ... your purse": The Elizabethan silver penny had a double cross and a crest stamped on the reverse, thus "bear no cross." In the 1983 SF production of *As You Like It* these lines were cut because of their relative obscurity.

lines 17 – 18:

"a young man ... solemn talk": These lines were cut.

line 35:

wearing was emended to *wearying*.

line 45:

"for coming a-night to Jane Smile" was changed to read "for sitting under Jane Smile's bum."

line 46:

batler was changed to *pail*.

line 49:

cods was changed to *peas*.

"giving her them again" was changed to "giving them to her."

lines 76 – 78:

"My master . . . hospitality": These lines were cut in order to expedite the action of the scene.

line 79:

"his cote, his flocks" was changed to "his cottage, flocks."

Act II / *Scene 5*

lines 23 – 25:

"and when . . . beggarly thanks": Jaques cynically derides the common courtesy of thanks as something one would expect from a beggar. These lines were cut.

line 50:

Ducdame: One of the most discussed passages in the play. A logical explanation is that the trisyllabic "ducdame" is a corruption of the Latin *duc ad me*, meaning "bring him to me" and thus paralleling the previous "come hither."

lines 58 – 59:

"his banquet . . . prepared": These lines were cut.

Act II / *Scene 6*

line 8:

"Thy conceit . . . powers": You fancy you are closer to death than you actually are.

Act II / *Scene 7*

line 6:

"discord in the spheres": It was thought that as the heavenly bodies moved around the earth they gave out a harmonious sound that mortals were too dull to hear.

lines 51 – 57:

"And why ... of the fool": Dr. Johnson again offers an explanation: "Unless men have the prudence not to appear touched with the sarcasms of a jester, they subject themselves to his power; and the wise man will have his folly 'anatomized', that is, dissected and laid open, by the 'squandering glances' or random shots of a fool."

lines 74 – 87:

"What woman ... But who comes here?" This speech is thought to have topical relevance, and may possibly allude to Ben Jonson or Jonson's enemy John Marston. Here Jaques speaks in the language of the satirists of the period, defending satire. These lines were cut in the 1983 SF production of *As You Like It*.

lines 127 – 28:

"Whiles ... food": These lines were cut.

lines 192 – 93:

"And as ... your face": These lines were cut.

Act III / *Scene 2*

line 2:

"thrice-crowned queen of night": In the words of Johnson: "alluding to the triple character of Proserpine, Cynthia and Diana, given by some mythologists to be the same goddess."

line 15:

naught was changed to *nothing*.
solitary was changed to *private*.

line 16:

private was changed to *solitary*.

lines 24 – 25:

"and that ... friends": These lines were cut.

lines 28 – 30:

"that he ... dull kindred": These lines were cut.

lines 36 – 37:

"all on one side" was changed to the simpler "half-baked."

line 51:

still was changed to *always*.
fells was changed to *fleece*.

lines 63 – 64:

"in respect ... indeed": Worm's meat means food for worms, i.e., a corpse. These lines were cut.

line 69

"God make incision in thee": There are two explanations. One is blood-letting to cure sickness; the other is "grafting to improve what is wild." This line was cut.

lines 94 – 95:

"it is . . . to market" was changed to "it sounds like a fat butter-woman ranting at market."

lines 104 – 05:

"They that . . . Rosalind": These lines were cut.

lines 114 – 15:

"I'll graff . . . medlar": A play on "you" as the yew tree and the "medlar" tree as a meddler. The fruit of the medlar rots before it is ripe.

lines 126 – 31:

"Some, how brief . . . and friend": These lines were cut in order to expedite the action of the scene.

lines 142 – 45:

Helen: The most beautiful woman of the ancient world: ". . . the face that launched a thousand ships." From *Dr. Faustus* by Christopher Marlowe.

Cleopatra: Famous Egyptian queen

Atalanta: Famous huntress and athlete. Her "better part" may be her physical prowess.

Lucretia: Faithful wife of Lucius Tarquinius Collatinus who stabbed herself to death when she was raped by Sextus Tarquinius.

lines 146 – 49:

"Thus Rosalind . . . priz'd": These lines were cut.

lines 172 – 73:

"be-rhym'd . . . rat": Johnson says humorously: "Rosalind is a very learned lady. She alludes to the Pythagorean doctrine which teaches that souls transmigrate from one animal to another, and relates that in his time she was an Irish rat, and by some metrical charm was rhymed to death. The power of killing rats with rhymes Donne mentions in his satires, and Temple in his treatises."

lines 180 – 81:

"hard matter . . . earthquakes": An allusion to the proverb "Friends may meet, but mountains never greet."

lines 222 – 24:

"to say . . . a catechism": These lines were cut to expedite the action of the scene.

line 242:

burden was changed to *chorus*.

lines 265 – 68:

The "pretty answers" Jaques refer to in line 265 are the poesies one would find inscribed on the inside of a gold ring. In line 267, *rings* was changed to *mottoes*. The "painted cloth" Orlando responds with in line 268 refers to cloth on which were painted serious scriptural and other texts. Though a more accessible wording for this passage was sought throughout the rehearsal process, one was never "discovered."

line 309:

a se'nnight was changed to *seven nights*.

lines 316 – 18:

"the one . . . penury": These lines were cut in order to expedite the action of the scene.

line 332:

cony was changed to *hare*.
kindled was changed to *born*.

line 342:

tax'd was changed to *charged*.

line 388:

"a dark house, and a whip": An Elizabethan punishment for the mad.

line 421:

After Rosalind said, "Will you go?" she repeated "sister."

Act III / *Scene 3*

lines 10 – 13:

"When a man's . . . a little room": This is considered a direct reference to Christopher Marlowe. The circumstances of Marlowe's death, in a quarrel over "le reckoninge" of a bill in a small private room in an inn, taken together with the line from his *The Jew of Malta*, "Infinite riches in a little room," seem to confirm this. In the 1983 SF production of *As You Like It* these lines were cut.

lines 47 – 59:

"But what though? . . . than to want": This long passage debating the "virtues" of wedded life and its horns of cuckoldry versus the "want" of the bachelor was cut in the 1983 SF production of the play.

line 60:

After "Here comes Sir Oliver" in the 1983 SF production, Touchstone called out "Sir Oliver."

line 61:

> After Touchstone's "Sir Oliver Martext" in the 1983 SF production, Martext responded "Hello . . . ah." As the character was being played as extremely nearsighted, his "hello" was to a tree and his "ah" to Touchstone.

line 70:

> *'ild* was changed to *yield*.

line 79:

> After Jaques said, "Get you to church," Martext interjected, "What?" in the 1983 SF production.

line 80:

> After Jaques said, "marriage is" in the 1983 SF production, Touchstone interjected "Sir Oliver."

line 88:

> After Jaques said, "counsel thee," Martext interjected "Ah" in the 1983 SF production.

line 90:

> After Touchstone said, "We must be married," Martext interjected, "Ah" in the 1983 SF production.

Act III / *Scene 4*

line 14:

> "He hath . . . lips of Diana": Diana was the patroness of virginity. See note for Act IV, *Scene I*, line 144. This line was cut in the 1983 SF production.

lines 38 – 41:

> "quite traverse . . . folly guides": Breaking a lance directly against an adversary's breast was considered honourable; but across it dishonourable, and an indication of ineptitude. These lines were cut as their meaning is relatively obscure.

Act III / *Scene 5*

line 11:

> "'Tis pretty . . . probable" was changed to "is it possible."

lines 22 – 24:

> "lean upon . . . moment keeps": These lines were cut.

lines 80 – 81:

> The "dead shepherd" is an allusion to Christopher Marlowe. "Who ever lov'd, that lov'd not at first sight?" is from Marlowe's *Hero and Leander*. See note for Act III, *Scene 3*, lines 10 – 13.

**Desmond Heeley and his assistant Polly Bohdanetzky fit
Wedding Scene costumes on actresses Seana McKenna and Jan Wood.**

lines 105 – 07:

"but I . . . master of": These lines were cut in order to expedite the action of the play. The information has already been given to the audience.

Act IV | *Scene 1*

line 18:

The second *my* is the generally accepted emendation for the Folio's *by*.

lines 31 – 36:

"Farewell, Monsieur . . . in a gondola": In the words of Johnson: "The fashion of travelling which prevailed very much in our author's time, was considered by the wise men as one of the principal causes of corrupt manners. It was therefore gravely censured . . . and is here, and in other passages ridiculed by Shakespeare." On *in a gondola*: "That is, . . . at Venice, the seat at that time of all licentiousness, where the young English gentlemen wasted their fortunes, debased their morals, and sometimes lost their religion." These lines were cut in the 1983 SF production of the play.

lines 79 – 82:

"Marry . . . of your suit": Rosalind's pun on suit as a "suit of clothes" and "courting," and possibly "lawsuit." These lines were cut in the 1983 SF production of the play.

line 90:

videlicet was cut.

line 129:

"I might . . . commission": Such a declaration, before a third party, constituted a kind of legal marriage contract; therefore this scene would have had even greater significance to the Elizabethan audience.

line 144:

"Diana in the fountain": Halliwell states: "The image of a fountain-figure weeping was an exceedingly common one, and . . . Diana was a favourite subject with the sculptors for such an object." One such fountain was erected in 1596 at Eleanor Cross in London.

Act IV / *Scene 3*

lines 44 – 49:

"Why, thy . . . a beast": These lines were cut.

line 77:

sheep-cote was changed to *cottage*.

line 78:

bottom was changed to *hollow*.

lines 86 – 88:

"and bestows . . . her brother": Due to the physical characteristics of the actresses playing Rosalind and Celia, these lines were changed to read "the woman tall and fairer than her brother." See note for Act I/*Scene 3*, line 11.

line 100:

"Within an hour": Orlando said, "For these two hours" in Act IV/ *Scene 1*, line 167, but no emendation seems necessary, as "one" can be defended as the indefinite article.

line 102:

"Lo, what . . . eye aside": This line was cut.

line 138:

By and by was cut.

Act V / *Scene 1*

lines 31 – 35:

"The heathen . . . lips to open": Possibly William's mouth is gaping open in astonishment, and Touchstone is confusing him further with his reference to a "heathen philosopher" (which we may assume is not a true reference). These lines were cut in the 1983 SF production of *As You Like It*.

Act V / *Scene 2*

line 27:

swoon is the generally accepted emendation for the Folio's *sound*.

lines 54 – 60:

"that I know . . . strange things": Rosalind flatters Orlando in order to persuade him of her magical powers. This polite address was cut in the 1983 SF production of the play.

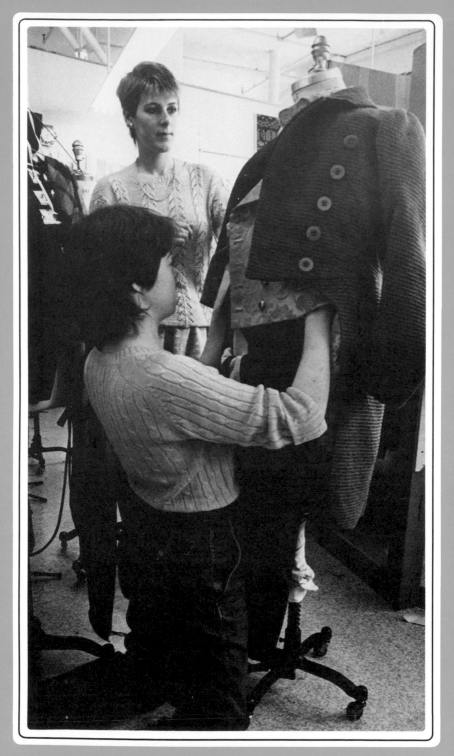

Festival wardrobe manager Louise Champion and seamstress
Diane Robinson working on Touchstone's costume for Lewis Gordon.

line 63:

> *damnable*: A probable reference to the Elizabethan Act against "Conjuracons, Inchantmentes and Witchecraftes," which enacted heavy punishment for those convicted of witchcraft.

line 71:

> "I tender dearly": A magician would have led a perilous life.

Act V | *Scene 4*

line 46:

> "undone three tailors": bankrupted them by not paying them.

lines 63 – 64:

> *dulcet diseases*: Does this phrase refer to "wits or witty people; so call'd because the times were infested with them," as Capell, a Shakespearean scholar stated, or "the sweet uneasiness of love, a time when people usually talk nonsense," as Dr. Farmer, another scholar, would read? Perhaps Johnson said it best: "This I do not understand. For diseases it is easy to read discourses; but perhaps the fault may lie deeper."

line 69:

> *courtier's beard*: The play *Sir Thomas More* was written sometime between 1596 and 1600, shortly preceding *As You Like It*. A portion of *Sir Thomas More* is attributed to Shakespeare. Is it possible that this comic discussion of a courtier's beard alludes to the most famous death in English history? As More put his head on the block at his execution he moved his beard aside, remarking that his "beard had done the king no offense." Pure conjecture, but, as always with Shakespeare, possible.

line 108:

> In the 1983 SF production Hymen was played by the same actor who portrayed Amiens.

Epilogue

lines 3 – 4:

> "good wine needs no bush": It was the custom to hang a tuft of ivy at the door of a vintner as an advertisement.

line 17:

> "If I were a woman": It was the custom in Shakespeare's day, of course, to have boy-actors playing the women's roles.

Biographical Notes

John Hirsch

Artistic Director John Hirsch directed *As You Like It* and *Tartuffe* for the 1983 Stratford Festival season. His other Stratford credits include *The Tempest* and *Mary Stuart*, 1982; *The Three Sisters*, 1976; *Hamlet* and *Satyricon*, 1969; *A Midsummer Night's Dream* and *The Three Musketeers*, 1968; *Richard III* and *Colours in the Dark*, 1967; *Henry VI*, 1966; and *The Cherry Orchard*, 1965.

Mr. Hirsch emigrated from Hungary to Canada in 1947. After graduating from the University of Manitoba he co-founded the Manitoba Theatre Centre and Winnipeg's Rainbow Stage. Former Consulting Artistic Director of the Seattle Repertory Theatre, he has staged productions at major theatres in North America, including the Guthrie Theater in Minneapolis.

He has won the Outer Circle Critics' Award for *St. Joan* at the Lincoln Center Repertory Theater, New York; an Obie Award for *AC-DC* at Brooklyn's Chelsea Theatre; and the Los Angeles Drama Critics' Award for *The Dybbuk* at the Mark Taper Forum, a work he also translated and adapted, and which brought him the Canadian Authors' Association Literary Award. His latest production at the Mark Taper was *Number Our Days*. He has also directed Verdi's *The Masked Ball* at the New York City Opera and Joseph Heller's *We Bombed in New Haven* on Broadway.

As former head of CBC Television Drama, Mr. Hirsch developed many outstanding drama projects, among them *A Gift to Last*, for which he received the Prix Anik Award; *For The Record*; *King of Kensington*; and *Sarah*, starring Zoe Caldwell, which was nominated for an International Emmy Award.

Mr. Hirsch is a member of the Order of Canada.

Desmond Heeley

In 1983 Desmond Heeley created designs for *As You Like It* and *The Country Wife*, which marked his 25th production for the Stratford Festival since 1957. He also designed the stage itself for the Third Stage. During his illustrious career Mr. Heeley has worked for most major theatre, opera, and ballet companies throughout Europe, Canada, and the United States, and won two Tony Awards for the Broadway production of *Rosencrantz and Guildenstern* in 1967. His most memorable Festival productions include *Arms and the Man*, 1982; *Coriolanus*, 1981; *Titus Andronicus*, 1978-80; *She Stoops to Conquer*, 1972-73; *The Duchess of Malfi*, 1971; *Cyrano*, 1962; and *Hamlet*, 1957.

His most current work includes Lance Mulcahy's *Sweet Will* in Toronto, a "marvellous" musical cabaret of Shakespeare's songs; and a new production of *La Sylphide* for Eric Bruhn, Baryshnikov, and the American Ballet Theatre, which opened in New York in June, 1983.

Elliott Hayes

Elliott Hayes is the Assistant Literary Manager of the Stratford Festival. For the 1982 Festival Season he was assistant director of *Arms and the Man*, and editor and writer of additional material for *A Variable Passion*. In 1973 he was assistant director of *The Marriage Brokers* at Stratford. A Stratford native, Mr. Hayes trained for three years at the Bristol Old Vic Theatre School in England. He was co-director of *The Caucasian Chalk Circle* and *A Midsummer Night's Dream* for the Verde Valley School in Arizona. Mr. Hayes has staged readings of original poetry, and his play *Summer and Fall* was workshopped at Stratford in 1981. In the 1983 Stratford season his play, *Blake*, was presented on the Third Stage, with Douglas Campbell in the *tour-de-force* role. Mr. Hayes is co-editor of the Stratford Festival Editions of *The Tempest*, *Macbeth*, *As You Like It*, and *The Taming of the Shrew*.

Michal Schonberg

Michal Schonberg is the Literary Manager of the Stratford Festival. His responsibilities include all the literary matters of the theatre, contacts with playwrights, scholars, and lecturers, as well as consultation on repertory. He is also co-editor of the Stratford Festival Editions of *The Tempest*, *Macbeth*, *As You Like It*, and *The Taming of the Shrew*. Associate Professor of Drama and Co-ordinator of Drama Studies at Scarborough College, University of Toronto, Mr. Schonberg has translated several works from Czech into English. He has also translated two of Tom Stoppard's plays, *Every Good Boy Deserves Favour* and *Professional Foul*, into Czech. He co-edited John Hirsch's adaptation of *The Dybbuk*, for publication and has had several works and adaptations published in *World Literature Today* and *Modern Drama*. Mr. Schonberg prepared the 1983 Stratford version of *Mary Stuart* with translator Joe McClinton.